ON GUARD, AMERICA
A Challenge To Islam

ON GUARD, AMERICA
A Challenge To Islam

- Forcing The Enemy Out From Within -

Why The Muslim Brotherhood Will Fail!

Kalai-o-Waha

authorHOUSE®

AuthorHouse™
1663 Liberty Drive
Bloomington, IN 47403
www.authorhouse.com
Phone: 1-800-839-8640

Published by AuthorHouse 2/13/2012

ISBN: 978-1-4567-9595-5 (sc)
ISBN: 978-1-4567-9593-1 (e)

Library of Congress Control Number: 2011916092

Books are available in quantity for promotional or premium use.
Write to Team OGA, Director of Sales, www.teamoga.com.

ACKNOWLEDGEMENTS

Organizing the contents of this book was going to be a relatively simple undertaking. Reading three different versions of the Quran and a dozen books on the subject of Islam, I was prepared to write about all the flaws I found in the Quran and in the ideology of Islam.

The contents were going to include the Understanding of Islam, the troubling pictures sent to me of Islamic activities, Creating A Religion and the Challenge To Islam. But, the more I wrote, the more information flowed to me, thereby increasing the amount of information necessary to tell this story.

Sadly, learning how erratic Muslims are by virtue of their role models and their influence from the Quran and the Madrassas, they tend to become violent, because that's the way they were taught.

Chapter 1
Introduction
My favorite talk show hosts and TV personalities

Chapter 2
A Few Of My Emails - "Cordoba House;"

Chapter 3
Understanding Islam
The three Qurans that I read were edited by
Abdel Haleem, Abdullah Yusuf Ali, Tarihke Tarsile

Chapter 4
Comparative Religions Of The World
Comparative Religions - The Encyclopedia of World Religions
By Robert D. Ellwood, General Editor, and Gregory D. Alles, Associate

Chapter 5
Minorities And Racial Differences

Chapter 6
Origin Of Terrorism
How Saudi Arabia Supports The New Global Terrorism.

Chapter 7
Jihad – Shariah Law – Caliphate
From the Encyclopedia of Religions – Mercia Eliade

Chapter 8
Can A Good Muslim Be A Good American?
"Muslims In The World," "Muslim Brotherhood," "Ikhwan,'
Dr. Peter Hammond – "A Quick Lesson On Islam,"
"All European Life Died In Auschwitz," "Australian Gun Update,"
"It's Time For Islamic State In America," Kitau In Mombasa,

Chapter 9
The Challenge
Yahweh (God) vs. Allah – Bible vs. Quran – Jesus vs. Muhammad
Team On Guard America's Challenge, Israel vs. Islam

Chapter 10
Show Islam The Way Out
Team 'On Guard, America' (TeamOGA) Company

Chapter 11
Take Heed America
"Exposing The Leftist Progressive Democrat Media;"
"I'm 63 and I'm Tired;" "A Black Man's Point Of View;"
"Mystery Man President;" "Marxism In America;"
"If George W. Bush;" Govt Sources – "In Two Years."

Chapter 12
If I Were President
Beating The Odds – Mission Statement
Other Things To Be Accomplished – DeIndustrialization of America
"Get Out Of Our House," "Differences In Compensation,"
Shame On Them

Chapter 13
Saving America
We The People – Big Kahuna Plan – Why We Will Win
A Thought – Third Party Candidate – Suicide Letter

To Kamalii Puanani, my wife and partner, with deepest love,

And to my children, *me ke aloha*, trying desperately to protect me.

Pohaku

Kaoleioku

Mokihana

Keikaha

Kanaina

Maile

Moku

Kawika

Kohu

Kamalii

Lokelani

And to my grand children, their children and future families:

This book was written especially for you - to ensure that you will come to enjoy the freedoms of the America I grew up in. I pray that we succeed in "Forcing Out The Enemy From Within" and taking back the White House and the Senate to Save America.
Malama Pono!

Table of Contents

CHAPTER 1   **INTRODUCTION** 1

CHAPTER 2   **A FEW OF MY EMAILS** 9

CHAPTER 3   **UNDERSTANDING ISLAM** 17

CHAPTER 4   **COMPARATIVE RELIGIONS OF THE WORLD** 35

CHAPTER 5   **MINORITIES AND RACIAL DIFFICULTIES** 61

CHAPTER 6   **ORIGIN OF TERRORISM** 79

CHAPTER 7   **JIHAD - SHARIAH LAW - CALIPHATE** 95

CHAPTER 8   **CAN A GOOD MUSLIM BE A GOOD AMERICAN?** . .105

CHAPTER 9   **THE CHALLENGE** 117

CHAPTER 10 **SHOW ISLAM THE WAY OUT** 135

CHAPTER 11 **AMERICA – TAKE HEED** .149

CHAPTER 12 **IF I WERE PRESIDENT** 153

CHAPTER 13 **SAVING AMERICA** 163

Chapter 1
Introduction

ON GUARD, AMERICA!

Help Me To Understand Why
I Would Want To Be A Muslim

When

My Options Of Befriending Anyone Are To:

Encourage Him/Her
To Become A Muslim,

OR

Warn Him/Her of Becoming A Slave
If He/She Doesn't Become A
Muslim,

OR

Kill Him/Her (The Infidel)
As Directed By The Quran.

WHAT?

THAT'S A RELIGION?

ARE YOU KIDDING ME?

NO JOKE!

IT REALLY DOES EXIST!

NOT ONLY DOES IT EXIST

BUT ITS MEMBERS PROMISE TO DESTROY AMERICA

Faisal Shahzad, the "Times Square Bomber," said
"The defeat of America is imminent and will happen in the near future.
We are only Muslims ... but if you call us Terrorists, we are proud
Terrorists and we will keep on terrorizing America.

We are only Muslims ....defending our
religion, people, homes and land."

Who Do They Think They Are?

What Are We Doing About That?

We're Going Into An

Attack Mode

Follow Me

I'll Show You How!

About The Author

Who Am I?   No one of significance.

I am a Cosmopolitan from Hawaii - A wounded combat veteran.

I know the pains associated with confrontations. I am a Tea Partier.

I didn't make much noise in 2010, and I am sorry about that. I plan to make a lot of noise now!

Why Am I Writing This Book?   Frustration Over Islam.

I have been inundated with emails and literature regarding the subject of Muslims planning to take over America to the point of raging frustration. Who do they think they are? I went to the library to get the answers, and the more I learned, the more frustrated I became. I will share some of my emails with you in the chapters that follow.

Why Would Anyone Read My Story? To Save America.

I want to share my story with my fellow Americans and Patriots. I want to tell them what I learned about Islam and develop a scenario to portray them the way I see them. Hopefully, my fellow Americans will share my frustrations and take a stand to stop the spread of this disease – Islam, to save America. It's not too late to apply a tourniquet to this injury.

Writing This Book

I agonized about putting my name on this book. I was concerned about my family being attacked by the evil forces I talk about.

Kalaimanaokahoowaha (translated: brilliant orator – chief negotiator) was a Warrior Prince, an uncle to King Kamehameha The Great of Hawaii. He served as a member of the King's War Council. He was skilled in the Hawaiian art of Lu'a, where they can literally dismantle their foes with their bare hands. I am a proud descendant of the Warrior Prince.

I am not a writer. I have written three other books, but they were all about me and my siblings; about my family heritage; about my combat experiences.

I have read many books by authors who were well versed in their subject matter and were able to present their facts authoritatively. All had mixed mannerisms, but for the most part, they were articulate. I make no such claim.

I enjoy reading what Rush Limbaugh publishes every month. I love the way he would masterfully disassemble his foes then charges on without leaving a bruise. Often I would say to myself: "How is it that he commands such a mastery of prose and so eloquently states his case when he didn't graduate from college?

I started out with the thought of articulating Rush's mannerisms by dazzling you with my literary prowess, but decided that I would not be able to keep up the guise, so I think I would do best being me. So, you will have to suffer through this subject matter with the way I write.

Kala mai i'au. (Sorry)

About The Subject - Islam
My email address has been flooded with letters from people all over the country about some scary stuff that is about to take place in America.

I've been reading all of these emails and kept wondering of their validity. Why are all these people running scared? Is there any truth to what they are saying? How can we, in America, be threatened by Islam? America was founded on Christian beliefs.

I decided to go to the library to check on Islam, the Muslims and the Quran.

The Analysts

Once this book is in circulation, there will be an army of analysts that will be called upon by the media, or the Liberals on the Hill, or unknowns looking for a chance to hit the big time, who will be volunteering to make comments about "Why I wrote this book."

Many of the analysts will side with Islam because they are afraid of disturbing what they perceive as seemingly good international relations. Others will think that I am an old battle torn veteran and that I am not capable of verbalizing common rationale.

It matters little to me what the analysts think. What is really important to me is that the members of the Tea Party read this book, and understand its contents.

As for the rest of the people of America, if you miss everything I say in this book, try to remember one thing:

We are at war with an enemy which, for some odd reason, is not yet identified by the President and his Administration;

An enemy whose roots are the biggest threat to America's security;

An enemy that is ruthless and evil and knows no good;

An enemy that is the Mother of Terrorism; and,

An enemy that must be stopped, at all cost.

Chapter 2
A Few of My Emails

New York City, NY

I received three emails showing a mass of Muslims gathered on Madison Avenue and 42nd Street and at 94th Street and 3rd Avenue, in New York City, New York.

With a total disregard for the civilian populace of Americans, the Muslims would gather on tarps to pray to Allah, while blocking traffic and business.

A Christian Nation cannot put up a Christmas scene of the baby Jesus in a public place, but the Muslims can stop traffic every Friday afternoon between 2PM and 4PM by worshipping in the streets.

Something is happening in America that is reminiscent of what is happening in Europe.

This is Political Correctness gone crazy.

It happens every Friday afternoon in several locations throughout NYC where there are mosques with a large number of Muslims that cannot fit into the mosque. They fill the surrounding streets, facing east, the direction of Mecca.

Palestine

Then, there were 24 photos sent of Palestinian children. The first three showed children cradled and crying because of the retaliation bombing by Israel with a caption – "The World Is Concerned About Palestinian Kids!" "These are the pictures that Al Jazeera shows."

The other 21 pictures have the caption "These are the pictures that they won't show you." It shows the children being trained by adult cadres on how to shoot all the weapons that could terrorize their neighbors.

9

Finally, there is a picture of a young lad with a grenade in his hand poised to throw it. On the bottom of that picture is a caption –

ENEMIES ARE A RENEWABLE RESOURCE
This is where our Government wants to send millions of dollars to help them rebuild Gaza . . . or is it to REARM?????

Vienna, Austria

There were videos sent of scenes in Vienna showing radical Muslims dancing in the streets waving long knives, like bayonets, in the air and periodically tapping the knife on the top of their head opening a wound to allow blood to flow down their faces.

The Muslim women were shown gathered on the side of the street watching the men going through their celebration.

Then, children were brought out on the streets and tapped on their heads with the knives to allow blood to flow down their faces.

It was disgusting enough to watch these radical idiots performing their dance with blood flowing down their faces, but with the children, who didn't particularly look like they were enjoying it, one was even crying, and the women looked on, emotionless.

Statement on the Proposed "Cordoba House"

There was an article written by Newt Gingrich. You may Google it by going to the Cordoba House.

The former Speaker of the House declared that "the time to take a stand is now – at this site on this issue – There should be no mosque near Ground Zero in New York so long as there are no churches or synagogues in Saudi Arabia. The time for double standards that allow Islamists to behave aggressively toward us while they demand our weakness and submission is over."

Mr. Gingrich explains that the destruction of one of our most famous landmarks is a test of the timidity, passivity and historic ignorance of American elites who don't understand that the "Cordoba House" is a deliberately insulting term. It refers to Cordoba, Spain – the capital of Muslim conquerors who symbolized their victory over the Christian Spaniards by transforming a church there into the world's third largest mosque complex.

Today, some of the Mosque's backers insist this term is being used to "symbolize interfaith cooperation" when, in fact, every Islamist in the world recognizes Cordoba as a symbol of Islamic conquest. It is a sign of their contempt for Americans and their confidence in our historic ignorance that they would deliberately insult us this way.

He goes on to say that if the people behind the Cordoba House were serious about "religious toleration they would be imploring the Saudis, as fellow Muslims, to immediately open up Mecca to all and immediately announce their intention to allow non-Muslim houses of worship in the Kingdom.

He closes with:

No mosque. No self-deception. No surrender. No way.

Confronting an Islamic Imam

This is a true story and the author is a well-known leader in prison ministry.

The man who walks with God always gets to his destination.
If you have a pulse you have a purpose.

The Muslim religion is the fastest growing religion per capita in the United States, especially in the minority races!

The Minister attended an annual training session that's required for maintaining his state prison security clearance. During the training session there was a presentation by three speakers representing the Roman Catholic, Protestant and Muslim faiths, who explained each of their beliefs.

The Minister was particularly interested in what the Islamic Imam had to say. The Imam gave a great presentation of the basics of Islam, complete with a video.

After the presentations, time was provided for questions and answers.

When it was his turn, the Minister directed his question to the Imam and asked:

'Please, correct me if I'm wrong, but I understand that most Imams and clerics of Islam have declared a holy jihad *[Holy war]* against the infidels of the world and, that by killing an infidel, *(which is a command to all Muslims)* they are assured of a place in heaven. If that's the case, can you give me the definition of an infidel?'

There was no disagreement with his statements and, without hesitation, the Imam replied, 'Non-believers!'

The Minister responded, 'So, let me make sure I have this straight. All followers of Allah have been commanded to kill everyone who is not of your faith so they can have a place in heaven. Is that correct?'

The expression on the Imam's face changed from one of authority and command to that of a little boy who had just been caught with his hand in the cookie jar.'

He sheepishly replied, 'Yes.'

The Minister then stated, 'Well, sir, I have a real problem trying to imagine Pope John Paul commanding all Catholics to kill those of your faith or Dr. Stanley ordering all Protestants to do the same in order to guarantee them a place in heaven!'

The Imam was speechless!

He continued, 'I also have a problem with being your friend when you and your brother clerics are telling your followers to kill me!

Let me ask you a question: Would you rather have your Allah, who tells you to kill me in order for you to go to heaven, or my Jesus who tells me to love you because I am going to heaven and He wants you to be there with me?'

You could have heard a pin drop as the Imam hung his head in shame. Needless to say, the organizers and/or promoters of the Diversification training seminar were not happy with the Minister's way of dealing with the Islamic Imam, and exposing the truth about the Muslims' beliefs.

In twenty years there will be enough Muslim voters in the U.S. to elect the President!

This Is Something Everyone Needs To Know!

(From a concerned citizen of Fresno, CA)
We now live about 30 miles from Fresno, CA. We are up in the Sierras and Fresno is the first big town we encounter when we leave the mountains. We shop there often. I received this from my ex-homicide partner who is still active in law enforcement circles in the Fresno area.

If you weren't at Rotary Friday, you missed the only decent speaker we've had in more than a year – a Lieutenant Colonel (LTC) from Fighter Wing's anti-terrorism office - who had a two-part presentation. First part was describing his job as the unit's anti-terrorism officer. It was pretty standard stuff.

The second part was information that will curl your hair. A Part-time air guardsman works as a checker at local Von's. Two women in full burkas buy every pre-paid cellphone in the store. Clerk (airman) gets to thinking about it. He goes to LTC and reports the incident. LTC asks store for surveillance video. It's scary enough that he contacts Fresno FBI.

FBI investigates and determines these women have been doing this all over the Valley. Cell phones shipped through Canada to Iraq/Afghanistan where they become triggers for roadside bombs.

The Shell station at Peach and Shaw. Every time a local GI goes there in fatigues he is asked specific questions. What is your unit? When are you deploying? How many aircraft are you taking?

The F-16s out of Fresno fly CAP for west coast. As such they are the first line of defense so they have the US 's most sophisticated air-to-air missiles. Foreign governments would like to get their hands on those missiles or at least learn how to build them. Also how many we have, etc. Two spy groups are working on it, one based at Fashion Fair Mall (the F-16s take-off pattern) and one based at Sierra Vista Mall (the F-16s landing pattern.)

LTC said the Ragheads *(But we don't profile.)* are always probing the base. Two dorks in a pickup show up at the front gate wanting to deliver a package marked Air National Guard, Fresno. No postage, no UPS, no FedEx, no DHL, no nothing. Just a probe.

I asked LTC why we haven't seen anything about this in The Bee, on KMJ, on local TV news. He said they're not interested. Since Friday I've learned of two other things. My brother-in-law Frank, (management at Avaya) had a Muslim tech who took a leave-of-absence for 6 weeks in Afghanistan. After the 6 weeks were up he called from New York requesting an extension. Frank (who does profile) said, you're fired, and called the Fresno FBI.

A Muslim who owns a liquor store in my former hometown of Kingsburg was constantly bugging customers to buy guns for him. Finally one of the guys I grew up with called the FBI.

We are a country at war and the enemy is among us. I don't care what Janet Napolitano says, it's a fight to the death and we should be prepared as possible. Brother-in-law Frank has a theory and I think it may be closer to the truth than Homeland Security wants to admit.

Two items of interest: The Sheriff wants to grant concealed carry permits to all who are qualified. A Columnist, among the most bleeding of the bleeding heart liberals, says it's time for Fresno residents to arm themselves. LOAD up, you can bet this is happening in places other than Fresno

Alliance of Patriots - Jihad Conference In Jerusalem

A speech was delivered by Geert Wilders, Chairman, Netherlands. You may Google it by the author's name.

Mr. Wilders starts out with, "I come to America with a mission. All is not well in the old world. There is a tremendous danger looming, and it is very difficult to be optimistic. We might be in the final stages of the Islamization of Europe. This not only is a clear and present danger to the future of Europe itself, it is a threat to America and the sheer survival of the West – the United States as the last bastion of Western civilization, facing an Islamic Europe."

He goes on to say that we have probably seen the landmarks. But in all of these cities, sometimes a few blocks away from tourist destination, there is another world. It is the world of the parallel society created by Muslim mass-migration.

All throughout Europe a new reality is rising: entire Muslim neighborhoods where very few indigenous people reside or are even seen. And if they are, they might regret it. This goes for the police as well. It is the world of head scarves, where women walk around in figureless tents, with baby strollers and a group of children. Their husbands, or slave holders, walk three steps ahead. There are mosques on many street corners. The shops have signs that you cannot read.

What he described are Muslim ghettos controlled by religious fanatics and they are mushrooming in every city across Europe. These are the building-blocks for territorial control of increasingly larger portions of Europe, street by street, neighborhood by neighborhood, city by city.

SUMMARY

Right from the start, you can see what upset me and why I thought it necessary to call attention to the things I learned about Islam.

In Chapter 2, of interest are:
Enemies Are A Renewable Source.
"This is where our government wants to send millions of dollars to help rebuild Gaza . . . or is it to Re-arm?"
Statement on Proposed Cordoba House – by Newt Gingrich. A terrific article about why a Mosque should not be built on Ground Zero. Why are there no Christian Churches or Synagogues in Saudi Arabia?

Confronting an Islamic Imam.
"I have a problem with being your friend when you and your brother clerics are telling your followers to kill me!"

Something Everyone Needs To Know
Women of Islam are gathering information from soldiers and buying cell phones as trigger devices to use against our troops in Afghanistan.

Speech by Geert Wilders, Party for Freedom, the Netherlands
"Liberty is the most precious of gifts. My generation never had to fight for this freedom. It was offered to us on a silver platter, by people who fought for it with their lives. All throughout Europe, American cemeteries remind us of the young boys who never made it home, and whose memory we cherish. "
Google that speech by Geert Wilders, especially if you feel that I did not build a strong enough case against Islam to identify them as a threat to America and against the world.
Mr. Wilders speech summarizes all my research and findings to put this book together. The only thing he left for me was to demand that Islam be removed from America while their population is at a number that we can overcome.
I agree with Mr. Wilders closing comment that "We have to take the necessary action now to stop this Islamic stupidity from destroying the free world that we know."
Note: You can speed read this book by going to the end of each chapter and reading the Summaries.
You will find them on pages 34, 60, 78, 94, 104, 115 and 133.

Chapter 3
Understanding Islam

General

I was familiar with the top ten Religions of the World. I have presented Sunday School Lessons on the subject of Comparative Religions of the World, except for Islam. Islam was not really known to me until now. But, having read the most recommended books on the subject, I can present their pros and cons, as well.

The books that were recommended to me, by the Library staff, were great read and excellent choices. I learned an awful lot and, now, I am a bit curious about Islam. For the most part, I have found the literature to be disturbing. I was at odds as to whether the authors exercised due diligence on the authenticity of Islam.

Of the three Qurans I read, the authors were all in concurrence about the uniqueness of the composition, the language and the classic nature of the books.

Before I decided to write this book, there were a number of questions I had about Islam the most important being,

What's the difference between

a Muslim and a Radical Muslim?
Or, a Muslim and a Muslim Terrorist?
Or, a Good Muslim and a Bad Muslim?

The Religion is called Islam, and its members are Muslims.
With the Radicals and Terrorists running rampant in Europe and in

America, it seems to me that Islam would do well to change the name of its members to Muhammadans or Islamists.

The name Muslim could then be used to identify terrorists. Therefore, there would be no Good Muslims. They would all be Radical, Terrorists and Bad

Before I go any further, I refer to the God of Abraham, the God of David, the God of Israel and the God of Christianity as - GOD.

I call the Supreme, Creator, the Originator, the Mighty, the Wise One, the Merciful, the all knowing, the Modeller, the all Powerful One according to the Quran – ALLAH.

God And Allah Are Not The Same.
My God Would Not Ask Me To Kill Anyone
Who Doesn't Believe In The Bible.

In America, we are mindful of all religions who are worshipping their own Gods with their religion in America. They can do this anywhere they wish.

When Islam entered America, it did not encounter any problems from the leaders of the other faiths in America.

Why would anyone be disturbed with that? If the U.S. government gives its blessing to a religion, why is that wrong? *(This is a trick question.)*

Correct Me If I'm Wrong

It is the goal of Islam to convert the entire world to the Islamic faith. If the people do not wish to convert, they are Unbelievers and are to be destroyed.

Once an area is declared a Muslim area *(Muslim state, Muslim country)* the other religions will not be able to establish their religion in that area. If they do, they will be destroyed.

The Imams play an active role in the politics of the Arab world. They are regarded as leaders in the community that establishes itself as a Muslim area.

By converting the majority of the people in America to Islam, then Islam, through its voting power, can control America.

At the current rate of growth, through conversion, it is estimated that within eight (8) years, America could be an Islamic country.

If that's the case, those who did not convert *(Unbelievers)*, will be destroyed.

There are no Christian Churches in Mecca, the religious capitol of Islam.

According to the Quran, Allah does not consent to the handling, preparation or consumption of swine

When a Luau is conducted, where the pig is roasted in a ground oven *(imu),* the whole area is considered contaminated and, therefore, Islam will not conduct business of any sort on that contaminated area.

There Are Questions

What about Freedom of Religion? Why can't other people of the world follow their own religion in their own country? Or in any country they wish to worship their God?

If I don't agree with the Quran or the books I have read about Islam, does it mean that I must be killed as an Infidel, *a Non-Believer* ?

America allows the Muslims to build their Mosques all over the USA to worship Allah. Will there be a time in the future that Islam will allow a Christian church to be built in Mecca?

Will we know when America is no longer an American State?

The Quran

In the introduction of the Quran, a comment is made that it is the infallible Word of Allah, a transcript of a tablet preserved in heaven, revealed to the Prophet Muhammad by the Angel Gabriel. Except in the opening verses and some few passages in which the Prophet or the Angel speaks in the first person, the speaker throughout is Allah.

In reading the Quran, there were many items that I questioned. I decided to list the items that disturbed me in alphabetical subject order.

My concerns, comments and arguments are contained in Chapter 9, The Challenge, written for the reader, not necessarily for Muslims, although I honestly believe it would help them, the Muslims, to understand their religion a lot better if they would read this book.

Believers

Believers, retaliation is decreed for you in bloodshed: a free man for a free man, a slave for a slave, and a female for a female. (Sura 2:178)

Believers, if you yield to a group from among those who were given the Book *(Bible),* they will turn you back from faith to unbelief. (Sura 3:101)

Believers, do not make friends with any but your own people (Sura 3:118)

Believers, if you yield to the infidels they will drag you back to unbelief and you will return headlong to perdition but Allah is your protector. He is the best of helpers. (Sura 3:149)

Believers, do not approach your prayers when you are drunk, but wait till you can grasp the meaning of your words; nor when you are unclean – unless you are travelling the road – until you have washed yourselves. (Sura 4:41)

If these *(Unbelievers)* do not keep their distance from you, lay hold of them and *kill them* wherever you find them. Over such men We give you absolute authority. (Sura 4:91)

It is unlawful for a Believer to kill another Believer, accidents excepted. He that accidentally kills a believer must free *one Muslim slave* and pay blood-money to the family of the victim, unless they choose to give it away in alms. (Sura 4:92)

Blessed are the believers, who are humble in their prayers; who avoid profane talk, and give alms to the destitute; who restrain their carnal desires *(except with their wives and* slave girls, *for these are lawful to them: transgressors are those who lust after other than these)*; who are true to their trusts and promises, and diligent in their prayers. These are the heirs of Paradise; they shall abide in it forever. (Sura 23:1)

Believers, when believing women seek refuge with you, test them. Allah best knows their faith. If you find them true believers, do not return them to the infidels; they are not lawful for the infidels, nor are the infidels lawful for them. But hand back to the unbelievers the dowries they gave them. Nor is it an offence for you to marry such women, provided you give them their dowries. (Sura 60:10)

Jesus, Son of Mary

We gave *Jesus son of Mary* indisputable signs and strengthened him with the Holy Spirit. Had Allah pleased, those who succeeded them would not have fought against one another after the veritable signs had been given them. But they disagreed among themselves; some had faith and others had none. (Sura 2:233)

He *(Jesus)* shall preach to men in his cradle and in the prime of manhood, and shall lead a righteous life.

'Lord,' she *(Mary)* said, 'how can I bear a child when no man has touched me?'

He *(Angel)* replied: 'Even thus, Allah creates whom He will. When He decrees a thing He need only say: "Be," and it is. (Sura 3:46)

They *(Christians)* denied the truth and uttered a monstrous falsehood against Mary. They declared: 'We have put to death the Messiah, *Jesus son of Mary*, the apostle of Allah.' They did not kill him, nor did they crucify him, but they thought they did. (Sura 4:155)

People of the book *(Christians)*, do not transgress the bounds of your religion. Speak nothing but the truth about Allah. The Messiah, *Jesus son of Mary*, was no more than Allah's apostle and His Word which He cast to Mary: a spirit from Him. (Sura 4:171)

They *(Christians)* say: 'Allah has begotten a son.' Allah forbid! Self-sufficient is He. His is all that the heavens and the earth contain. Surely for this you have no sanction. Would you say of Allah what you know not? (Sura 10:67)

Say: 'Praise be to Allah who has never begotten a son; who has no partner in His Kingdom; who needs none to defend Him from humiliation.' (Sura 17:111)

We sent to her Our spirit in the semblance of a full-grown man. And when she saw him she said: 'May the Merciful defend me from you! If you fear the Lord, *(leave and go your way.)*'

'I am but your Lord's emissary,' he replied, 'and have come to give you a holy son.'

'How shall I bear a child,' she answered, 'when I have neither been touched by any man nor ever been unchaste?'

'Thus did your Lord speak,' he replied, '" That is easy enough for Me. He shall be a sign to mankind and a blessing from Ourself. This is Our decree."'

Thereupon she conceived him, and retired to a far-off place. And when she felt the throes of childbirth, she lay down by the trunk of a palm tree, crying: 'Oh, would that I had died before this, and passed into oblivion!' (Sura 19:17)

Carrying the child, she came to her people, who said to her: 'Mary, this is indeed a strange thing! Your father was never a whoremonger, nor was your mother a harlot.

She made a sign to them, pointing to the child. But they replied: 'How can we speak with a babe in the cradle?'

Whereupon he *(Jesus)* spoke and said: 'I am the servant of God. He has given me the Book and ordained me a prophet. His blessing is upon me where I go, and He has exhorted me to be steadfast in prayer and to give alms as long as I shall live. He has exhorted me to honour my mother and has purged me of vanity and wickedness. Blessed was I on the day I was born, and blessed I shall be on the day of my death and on the day I shall be raised to life.'

Such was *Jesus son of Mary.* That is the whole truth, which they still doubt. Allah forbid that He Himself should beget a son! When He decrees a thing He need only say: 'Be,' and it is. (Sura 19:27)

We sent forth Noah and Abraham, and bestowed on their offspring prophethood and the Scriptures. Some were rightly guided, but many were evil-doers. After them We sent other apostles, and after those *Jesus the son of Mary.* We gave him the Gospel, and put compassion and mercy in the hearts of his followers. As for monasticism, they instituted it themselves for We had not enjoined it on them, seeking thereby to please Allah; but they did not observe it faithfully. We rewarded only those who were true believers; for many of them were evil-doers.

Believers, have fear of Allah and put your trust in His apostle *(Muhammad).* He will grant you double share of His mercy, He will bestow on you a light to walk in, and He will forgive you: Allah is forgiving and merciful. (Sura 57:27)

Jews and Christians (Unbelievers – Infidels)

The Jews say that the Christians are misguided, and the Christians say it is the Jews who are misguided. Yet they both read the Scriptures. And the ignorant say the same of both. Allah will on the Day of Resurrection judge their disputes. (Sura 2:113)

When they *(Christians)* face their punishment those who were followed will disown their followers, and the bonds which now unite them will break asunder. Those who followed them will say: 'Could we but live again, we would disown them as they have now disowned us.'

Thus will Allah show them their own works. They shall sigh with remorse, but shall never emerge from the Fire. (Sura 2:166)

The only true faith in Allah's sight is Islam. Those to whom the Scriptures were given disagreed among themselves, through insolence, only after knowledge had been vouchsafed them. He that denies Allah's revelations should know that swift is Allah's reckoning. (Sura 3:19)

Allah made a covenant with the Israelites . . . But because they broke their covenant, We laid on them Our curse and hardened their hearts. (Sura 5:13)

With those who said they were Christians We made a covenant also, but they too have forgotten much of what they were exhorted to do. Therefore We stirred among them enmity and hatred, which shall endure till the Day of Resurrection, when Allah will declare to them all what they have done. (Sura 5:14)

Allah revealed His will to the angels, saying: 'I shall be with you. Give courage to the believers. I shall cast terror into the hearts of the infidels. Strike off their heads, strike off the very tips of their fingers!' (Sura 8:12)

None should visit the mosques of God except those who believe in Allah and the Last Day. (Sura 9:18)

The Jews say Ezra is the son of Allah, while the Christians say the Messiah is the son of Allah. Such are their assertions, by which they imitate the infidels of old. Allah confound them! How perverse they are. (9:30)

The Unbelievers among the People of the Book and the pagans did not desist from unbelief until the Proof was given them; an apostle from Allah reciting from purified pages infallible decrees.

Nor did those who were vouchsafed the Book disagree among themselves until the Proof was given them. Yet they were enjoined only to serve Allah and to worship none but Him, to attend to their prayers and to render the alms levy. That, surely, is the infallible faith.

The unbelievers among the People of the Book and the pagans shall burn forever in the fire of Hell. They are the vilest of all creatures. (Sura 98:6)

Kabah

Allah has made the Kabah the Sacred House, the sacred month, and the sacrificial offerings with their ornaments, eternal values for mankind; (Sura 5:97)

Life On Earth vs. Life After

Are you content with this life in preference to the life to come? Few are the blessings of this life, compared with those of the life to come. (Sura 9: 38)

Woe betide the unbelievers, for they shall be sternly punished! Woe betide those who love this life more than the life to come; who debar others from the path of Allah and seek to make it crooked. (Sura 14:3)

The Quran gives guidance to that which is most upright. It promises the faithful who do good work a rich recompense, and those who deny the life to come a woeful scourge. (Sura 17:9)

As for the righteous, they shall be lodged in peace together amid gardens and fountains, arrayed in rich silks and fine brocade. Even thus; and We shall wed them to dark-eyed houris. Secure against all ills, they shall call for every kind of fruit; and, having died once, they shall die no more. (Sura 44:49)

Make War

Make war on them: Allah will chastise them at your hands and humble them. He will grant you victory over them and heal the spirit of the faithful. He will take away all rancor from their hearts: Allah shows mercy to whom He pleases. Allah is all-knowing and wise. (Sura 9:`14)

Believers, make war on the infidels who dwell around you. Deal firmly with them. Know that Allah is with the righteous. (Sura 9:123)

When you meet the unbelievers in the battlefield strike off their heads and, when you have laid them low, bind your captives firmly. (Sura 47:4)

Muhammad – Jesus Claims Muhammad Will Follow Him?

And of *Jesus, son of Mary,* who said to the Israelites: 'I am sent forth to you from Allah to confirm the Torah already revealed, and to give news of an apostle that will come after me whose name is Ahmad.* (Sura 61:6)

(* Another name of Muhammad's, meaning 'The Praised One.')

Muhammad, we* are told, was once found by his wife, Hafsah, with a Coptic Slave from whom he had promised her to separate. Of this Hafsah secretly informed 'A'ishah, another wife of his. To free Muhammad from his promise to Hafsah was the object of this chapter. Some of the references are obscure. (Footnote after Sura 66:1)

Prophet, rouse the faithful to arms. If there are twenty steadfast men among you, they shall vanquish two hundred; and if there are a hundred, they shall rout a thousand unbelievers, for they are devoid of understanding. (Sura 8:65)

Prophet, We have made lawful for you the wives to whom you have granted dowries and the *slave girls whom Allah has given you as booty*; the daughters of your paternal and maternal uncles and of your paternal and maternal aunts who fled with you; and any believing woman who gives herself to the Prophet and whom the Prophet wishes to take in marriage. This privilege is yours alone, being granted to no other believer. (35:30)

By the declining star, your compatriot *(Muhammad)* is not in error, nor is he deceived. He does not speak out of his own fancy. This is an inspired revelation. He is taught by one who is powerful and mighty *(the Angel Gabriel)*. He stood on the uppermost horizon; then, drawing near, he came down within two bows' length or even closer, and revealed to his servant *(Muhammad)* that which he revealed.

We have given you *(Muhammad)* a glorious victory *(Taking of Mecca)*, so that Allah may forgive you your past and future sins, and perfect His goodness to you; (Sura 48:1)

Muhammad is Allah's apostle. Those who follow him are ruthless to the unbelievers but merciful to one another. (Sura 48:29)

His *(Muhammad's)* own heart did not deny his vision. How can you *(unbelievers)* question what he *(Muhammad)* sees? (Sura 53:1)

Muslims

This day I have perfected your religion for you and completed My favour to you. I have chosen Islam to be your faith. (Sura 5:3)

Believers, when you rise to pray wash your faces and your hands as far as the elbow, and wipe your heads and your feet to the ankle. If you are unclean, cleanse yourselves. (Sura 5:6)

Believers, when you encounter the infidels on the march, do not turn your back to them in flight. If anyone on that day turns his back to them, except for tactical reasons, or to join another band, he shall incur the wrath of Allah and Hell shall be his home: an evil fate. (Sura 8:16)

Some of us are Muslims and some are wrongdoers. Those that embrace Islam pursue the right path; but those that do wrong shall become the fuel of Hell. (Sura 72:14)

Paradise – Virgins – The Garden of Eden (for Believers)

As for those that have faith and do good works, We shall not deny them their reward. They shall dwell in the gardens of Eden, where rivers will roll at their feet. Reclining there upon soft couches, they shall be decked with bracelets of gold, and arrayed in garments of fine green silk and rich brocade: blissful their reward and happy their resting place! (Sura 18:30)

As for those that have faith and do good works, Allah will admit them to gardens watered by running streams. They shall be decked with bracelets of gold and of pearls, and arrayed in garments of silk. (Sura 22:23)

They shall enter the Gardens of Eden, where they shall be decked with bracelets of gold and pearls, and arrayed in robes of silk. They will say: 'Praise be to Allah who has taken away all sorrow from us. Our Lord is forgiving and bountiful in His rewards. (Sura 35:31)

But the true servants of Allah shall be well provided for, feasting on fruit and honored in the gardens of delight. Reclining face to face upon soft couches, they shall be served with a goblet filled at a gushing fountain, white, and delicious to those who drink it. It will neither dull their senses nor befuddle them. They shall sit with bashful, dark-eyed virgins, as chaste as the sheltered eggs of ostriches. (Sura 37:40)

The righteous shall return to a blessed retreat: the gardens of Eden, whose gates shall open wide to receive them. Reclining there with bashful virgins for companions, they will call for abundant fruit and drink. (Sura 38:50)

Enter Paradise, you and your spouses, in all delight. You shall be served with golden dishes and golden cups. Abiding there forever, you shall find all that your souls desire and all that your eyes rejoice in.

Such is the Paradise you shall inherit by virtue of your good deeds. Your sustenance shall be abundant fruit. (Sura 43:70)

Such is the Paradise which the righteous have been promised: therein shall flow rivers of water undefiled, and rivers of milk forever fresh; rivers of wine delectable to those that drink it, and rivers of clarified honey. There shall they eat of every fruit, and receive forgiveness from their Lord. (Sura 47:12)

But in the gardens the righteous shall dwell in bliss, rejoicing in what their Lord will give them. Their Lord will shield them from the scourge of Hell. He will say: 'Eat and drink to your hearts' content. This is the reward of your labours.

They shall recline on couches ranged in rows. To dark-eyed houris We shall wed them. Fruits We shall give them, and such meats as they desire. They will pass from hand to hand a cup inspiring no idle talk, no sinful urge; and there shall wait on them young boys of their own, as fair as virgin pearls.

They will converse with one another. 'When we were living among our kinsfolk,' they will say, 'we were troubled by many fears. But Allah has been gracious to us; He has preserved us from the fiery scourge, for we have prayed to Him. He is the Beneficent One, the Merciful. (Sura 52:15)

When the earth shakes and quivers - you shall be divided into three multitudes: (left, right and fore) From the fore – they shall be brought near to their Lord in the gardens of delight; a whole multitude from the men of old, but only a few from the latter generations.

They shall recline on jeweled couches face to face, and there shall wait on them immortal youths with bowls and ewers and a cup of purest wine (that will neither pain their heads nor take away their reason); with fruits of their own choice and flesh of fowls that they relish. And theirs shall be the *dark-eyed houris*, chaste as *virgin* pearls; a guerdon for their deeds. (Sura 56:1)

But for those that fear the majesty of their Lord, there are two gardens planted with shady trees. Each is watered by a flowing spring. Each bears every kind of fruit in pairs.

They shall recline on couches lined with thick brocade, and within reach will hang the fruits of both gardens.

Therein are bashful virgins whom neither man nor jinnee will have touched before - Virgins as fair as corals and rubies. (Sura 55:52)

Shall the reward of goodness be anything but good? And, beside there shall be two other gardens of darkest green.

A gushing fountain shall flow in each. Each planted with fruit trees, the palm and the pomegranate. In each there shall be virgins chaste and fair – dark-eyed virgins, sheltered in their tents, whom neither man nor jinnee will have touched before.

They shall recline on green cushions and fine carpets. Blessed be the name of your Lord, the Lord of majesty and glory! (Sura 55:67)

Punishment

The adulterer and the adulteress shall each be given a hundred lashes. Let no pity for them cause you to disobey Allah, if you truly believe in Allah and the Last Day; and let their punishment be witnessed by believers. (Sura 24:1)

The adulterer may marry only an adulteress or an idolatress; and the adulteress may marry only an adulterer or an idolater. True believers are forbidden such marriages. (Sura 24:3)

Those that defame honourable women and cannot produce four witnesses shall be given eighty lashes. Do not accept their testimony ever after, for they are great transgressors – except those among them that afterwards repent and mend their ways. Allah is forgiving and merciful. (24:4)

Quran (Koran)

This Quran could not have been devised by any but Allah. It confirms what was revealed before it and fully explains the Scriptures. It is beyond doubt from the Lord of the Universe. (Sura 10:34)

If they *(Unbelievers)* say: 'He *(Muhammad)* has invented it *(Koran)* himself,' say to them: 'Produce ten invented chapters like it. (Sura 11:13)

Those who are burdened with sin shall come to grief: but those who have believed and done good works shall fear no tyranny or injustice.

Thus have We sent it down: a Koran in the Arabic tongue, and proclaimed in it warnings and threats so that they may take heed and be admonished. (Sura 20:113)

Some say: 'The Quran is but a medley of dreams.' Others: 'He has invented it himself.' And yet others: 'He is a poet: let him show us some sign, as did the apostles in days gone by.' (Sura 21:5)

We have revealed the Quran in clear verses. Allah gives guidance to whom He will.

As for the true believers, the Jews, the Sabaeans, Christians, the Magians, and the pagans, Allah will judge them on the Day of Resurrection. (Sura 22:16)

These are the revelations of the Quran, a Glorious Book; a guide and joyful tidings to true believers, who attend to their prayers and render the alms levy and firmly believe in the life to come. (Sura 27:1)

Righteousness

Righteousness does not consist in whether you face the East or the West. The righteous man is he who believes in Allah and the Last Day, in the angels and the Book and the prophets; who, though he loves it dearly, gives away his wealth to kinsfolk, to orphans, to the destitute, to the traveler in need and to beggars, and for the redemption of captives; who attends to his prayers and renders the alms levy; who is true to his promises and steadfast in trial and adversity and in times of war. Such are the true believers; such are the God fearing. (Sura 2:177)

Sabbath

The Sabbath was ordained only for those who differed about it. On the Day of Resurrection your Lord will judge their disputes. (Sura 16:124)

Slaves

Show kindness to parents and kindred, to orphans and to the destitute, to near and distant neighbors, to those that keep company with you, to the traveler in need, and to the *slaves* you own. (Sura 4:36)

Enjoin believing women to turn their eyes away from temptation and to preserve their chastity; not to display their adornments (except such as are normally revealed); to draw their veils over their bosoms and not to display their finery except to their husbands, their fathers, their husband's fathers, their sons, their step-sons, their brothers, their brothers' sons, their sisters' sons, their women servants, and their *slave-girls;* male attendants lacking in natural vigour, and children who have no carnal knowledge of women. (Sura 24:31)

Take in marriage those among you who are single and those of your male and *female slaves* who are honest. If they are poor, Allah will enrich them from His own bounty. Allah is munificent and all-knowing. (Sura 34:32)

Those that divorce their wives by so saying, and afterwards retract their words, shall *free a slave* (as a penalty) before they touch each other again. This you are enjoined to do; Allah is cognizant of all your actions. (Sura 58:3)

Swine (Pork)

Believers, eat of the wholesome things with which We have provided you and thanks to Allah, if it is Him you worship.

He has forbidden you carrion, blood, and the flesh of swine, also any flesh that is consecrated other than in the name of Allah. (Sura 2:172)

Unbelievers (Infidels) - To Hell – The Fire - The Scourge

If you doubt what We have revealed to Our servant, produce one chapter comparable to it. Call upon your idols to assist you, if what you say be true. But if you fail (as you are sure to fail), then guard yourselves against the Fire whose fuel is men and stones, prepared for the unbelievers. (Sura 2:24)

And now that a Book *(Quran)* confirming their own has come to them from Allah, they deny it, although they know it to be the truth and have long prayed for help against the unbelievers. Allah's curse be upon the infidels! (Sura 2:89)

"Lord," said Abraham, "make this a secure land and bestow plenty upon its people, those of them that believe in Allah and the Last Day."

'As for those that do not,' He answered, 'I shall let them live awhile, and then shall drag them to the scourge of the Fire: an evil fate.' (Sura 2:126)

Those that deny Allah's revelations shall be sternly punished; Allah is mighty and capable of revenge. (Sura 3:4)

As for the unbelievers, neither their riches nor their children will in the least save them from Allah's judgment. They shall become the fuel of the Fire. (Sura 3:10)

As for the unbelievers, neither their riches nor their children shall in the least protect them from Allah's scourge. (Sura 3:116)

He whom Allah confounds, you cannot guide. They would have you disbelieve as they themselves have disbelieved, so that you may be all alike. Do not befriend them until they have fled their homes in the cause of Allah. If they desert you, seize them and put them to death. (Sura 4:89)

Children of Adam, when apostles of your own come to proclaim to you My revelations, those that take warning and mend their ways will have nothing to fear or to regret; but those that deny and scorn Our revelations shall be the heirs of the Fire, wherein they shall remain forever. (Sura 7:35)

He that fears Allah will heed it, but the wicked sinner will flout it. He shall burn in the gigantic Fire, where he shall neither die nor live. Happy shall be the man who keeps himself pure, who remembers the name of his Lord and prays. (Sura 87:10)

Women

Keep aloof from women during their menstrual periods and do not approach them until they are clean again; when they are clean, have intercourse with them whence Allah enjoined you. Allah loves those that turn to him in penitence and strive to keep themselves clean.

Women are your fields: go, then, into your fields whence you please. Do good works and fear Allah. (Sura 2:222)

Women shall with justice have rights similar to those exercised against them, although men have a status above women. Allah is mighty and wise. (Sura 2:228)

If you fear that you cannot treat orphan girls with fairness, then you may marry other women who seem good to you: two, three, or four of them. But if you fear that you cannot maintain equality among them, marry one only or any *slave-girls* you may own. This will make it easier for you to avoid injustice. (Sura 4:3)

A male shall inherit twice as much as a female. (Sura 4:11)

Men have authority over women because Allah has made the one superior to the other, and because they spend their wealth to maintain them.

Good women are obedient. They guard their unseen parts because God has guarded them. As for those from whom you fear disobedience, admonish them and forsake them in beds apart, and beat them. (Sura 4:34)

Women Of Islam

Why Would You Want To Be A Muslim If ALLAH:

Thinks you're not as important as a man?

Thinks that you are worth only half the inheritance of your brother?

Feels you need 4 male witnesses for a case against your husband if he mistreats you?

Tells your husband to BEAT you if you are not obedient?

The Sad Part Having read the literature about Islam, to include three versions of the Quran, I understand that the male members of Islam try desperately to keep the women *(Women of Islam)* from learning anything. They would feel threatened if the women were aware of their rights. The men have kept the women from being educated.

My hope is that, somehow, some intelligent woman can share the message of this book with the Women of Islam so that they can take advantage of the "streams running through their land" before they die and go to Paradise, as described in the Quran, in every chapter.

We can show the Women of Islam Paradise, here on earth, in their lifetime, just by freeing themselves of Islam. It doesn't matter whether they decide to be a Christian, Jew, Buddhist, Hindu, Shinto, Sikhist, Bahaiist, Judaist, Confucianist, Jainist, Taoist, or whatever.

Contrary To What You Heard I know that many Muslim women are opposed to the American lifestyle because of the way American women dress and flaunt their feminism in half-nude dress styles.

I'm assuming that that comment is criticizing the American Show-Girls – Strip Clubs.

My response would be that it would take a while before any female, not American, could adjust to the fashions of the west.

But, look at the positive side of things. As a female, you have the God-given right to look as beautiful as you are, or wish to be, instead of covering yourself from head to foot so no one will be able to see how beautiful you are.

Muslim men are very insecure. They have accepted the traditional Burka sent down from generation to generation because they don't want other men to see their women. That's sad.

Staying In America If you decide to stay in America, how you dress is entirely up to you. You don't have to look like the beautiful American women you seem to despise. Dress conservatively.

SUMMARY

God and Allah are not the same. "My God would not ask me to kill anyone who doesn't believe in the Bible."

Correct Me If I'm Wrong.
The goal of Islam is to convert the world to the Islamic faith.
Non-believers are Infidels and must be destroyed.
Converting the US to Islam, through votes, Islam controls America.
At the current rate of conversion, Islam could control America in 8 years.
Islam will not conduct business of any sort on contaminated ground.

The Quran
From the Quran, I decided to itemize all the things that I did not agree with then put them into subject categories in alphabetical order. After reading this chapter, you will probably have a number of questions which I may answer in Chapter 9, The Challenge.

Believers - Jesus, Son of Mary - Jews and Christians (Unbelievers – Infidels) – Kabah - Life On Earth vs. Life After - Make War

Muhammad, Jesus Claims Muhammad Will Follow Him? – Muslims, Paradise, Virgins, The Garden of Eden (for Believers) – Punishment – Quran – Righteousness – Sabbath – Slaves - Swine (Pork) - Unbelievers (Infidels), Going To Hell, The Fire, The Scourge – Women

Women of Islam - Why would you want to be a Muslim If Allah:
Thinks you're not as important as a man?
Or, Thinks you are worth only half of your brother?
Or, Tells your husband to Beat you if you are not obedient?
What kind of God is Allah?

Being An American Female
I share my views of the American woman on the previous page. Being conservative and a senior, I'm sure that the younger guys would probably have a whole lot more to say on this subject.

No Comments until the Challenge - Chapter 9

The next Summary is on Page 60.

Chapter 4

Comparative Religions Of The World

Introduction

In this Chapter, we take a look at the Religions of the World to find the key differences in beliefs. As stated in "Acknowledgements," the information was taken from Comparative Religions of the World by Robert D. Ellwood, General Editor, and Gregory D. Alles, Associate.

The Religions are listed by their sizes from the largest to the smallest. Accordingly, we are presenting the twelve best known religions of the world:

Christianity, (*Belief that Jesus was the Son of God, preached and performed miracles);*
Islam *(Mecca to Medina by Muhammad in Arabia - 622CE);*
Hinduism *(Indus Valley Religion of India - 3500-1500 BCE);*
Buddhism *(Siddhartha Gautama in Tibet – 560-480 BCE);*
Judaism *(Moses on Mt Sinai, Abraham in Israel 1800 BCE);*
Sikhism *(Guru Nanak in northwest India - 1469-1539 CE);*
Baha'iism *(Iran Bab "gateway" predicted the One to Come – Baha'ullah, in 1840);*
Confucianism*(Kung-tu-tzu "Master Kung" in China – sixth century BCE);*
Jainism *(Jina of India – 6th century BCE - ford makers);*
Shintoism *(Japanese religion, "way of the Gods" worship of Kami – 6th century BCE);*
Zoroastrianism *(Prophet Zarathustra of Iran – 6th century BCE – worship of Ahura Mazda);*

Taoism *(Chinese religion Lao Tzu "Old Master" 4th century BCE "the way of nature in things").*

Christianity   *2.1 Billion*

The religion centered on belief in Jesus as the Son of God. Although it has representatives throughout the globe, Christianity is especially prominent in Europe, the Americas, and Australia.

History: Jesus was a Jew who lived primarily in Galilee (northern Israel). It is said that he wandered the countryside, teaching and working Miracles. Pontius Pilate, the Roman governor of Judea (southern Israel) had him crucified on charges of sedition against the Roman government, but his followers soon became convinced that he had been raised from the dead. Some of these followers traveled as Missionaries, mostly throughout the Roman Empire. They taught that Jesus was the promised Messiah or Christ and that he provided people with forgiveness for their sins and eternal life.

Started in the year 35 AD, Christianity has grown and divided into 122 Denominations with over Two Billion Christians around the world.

Belief: Christians believe that Jesus Christ is Lord and Savior and preach Love and Peace.

Religious Doctrine: The Bible – Old Testament and New Testament. The first five books of the Old Testament were written by Moses. The other books were contributed by Disciples.

The New Testament was written by Matthew, Mark, John and Luke. The other books were added on by Paul others associated with Jesus. The Old Testament is a beautiful story of the beginning. The New Testament starts with the immaculate conception of Jesus, his birth which was announced by a Star from afar and the coming of the Three Wise Men. In His lifetime, He performed 34 Miracles before being crucified where Paul picks up the story and glorifies it with every new Chapter.

Ideology: The Bible is a story of Love and Peace.

Islam   *1.2 Billion*

Islam is Arabic for "submission." Specifically, submission to the will of God; a religion that took final form in Arabia after revelations to the prophet Muhammad (570-632 CE). People who practice the religion are called Muslims (earlier called Moslems).

History: Muslims call the time before the prophet Muhammad *al-*

Jahiliya. "the times of ignorance." At that time semi-nomadic herders, Caravaners, and towns people lived in Arabia. Their primary loyalty was to their clans, and their religions were polytheistic and local. The revelations to Muhammad proclaimed that human beings owed primary loyalty to the one true God, whom alone they should obey (Allah). As a result a new community, the Ummah of Islam, was created, based not on blood relationship but on shared Faith. Muslims date its existence from the *Hijra* (also spelled hegira), the flight of Muhammad and his followers from Mecca to Medina in 622.

After the prophet's death, the revelations he had received were collected and compiled into a book known as the Qur'an. Over the next 300 years, scholars collected stories of the prophet's deeds and sayings, the *Hadith*. At the same time, several schools of thought arose. The most important disagreement divided a minority of Muslims, known as Shi'ites from most other Muslims, known as Sunnis. Sunnis accepted the Umayyad dynasty, which ruled in Damascus, while Shi'ites claimed that the prophet's male descendants should lead the community of Islam.

Islam expanded rapidly. Within a century of the prophet's death, it extended from Spain and Morocco in the west through the Near East and Iran to central Asia in the east. In 750 the Abbasid dynasty succeeded the Umayyads and, ruling from Baghdad, presided over a magnificent civilization. During this period Islam developed sophisticated traditions of philosophy and profound schools of Mysticism, known as *Sufism*.

After the fall of the Abbasids in 1258, the Islamic world was divided among regional powers. The powerful Turks overthrew Constantinople in 1453 and lay siege to Vienna, Austria, in the 1520s and again in 1683. The Mughals produced great monuments of South Asian civilization, including the famed Taj Mahal, a mausoleum in Agra, India. From south Asia, Islam spread east to Indonesia, the most populous Islamic country today. In Africa south of the Sahara, Muslims also developed several long-lasting societies.

In the 18th and 19th centuries, European colonizers overran much of the Islamic world and ruled it until after World War II (1939-45). Some Muslims, including Turkish reformers, reacted by rejecting Islamic traditions as outmoded. They adopted a secular worldview informed by modern science. Others, like the south Asian poet Muhammad Iqbal (1877-1938), maintained that Islam provided a spiritual grounding for science. From the 1930s on in North America some African Americans found meaning in the teachings of Elijah Muhammad, who led an organization known as the

Nation of Islam; many Muslims in other parts of the world question whether Elijah Muhammad was actually teaching Islam.

At the beginning of the 21st century, Islam finds itself second only to Christianity in its number of active adherents among the religions of the world. The sharp decline in the practice of Buddhism and the other traditional religions of China after the communist triumph in 1949 contributed to Islam's status as the world's second-largest religion.

Moreover, seldom in the history of the religions of the world has the outer status of a religion changed as dramatically as has Islam since the beginning of the 20th century. In 1900, most Muslims lived under the humiliating colonial rule of professedly Christian overlords – British, French, Dutch, or Russian - or in weak and backward Muslim empires, the Ottoman and Persian. Most of the Muslim world was sunk in poverty and underdeveloped. Many, among, both Muslims and non-Muslims, had a sense that Islamic culture was stagnant, its day perhaps past.

In 2000, the situation was radically different virtually all Muslim societies were independent nations by then, and some had become wealthy and technologically advanced, mostly from oil revenue. Vibrant new Islamic cultural and political movements insisted that, far from dead, Islam was a contemporary way of life that had much to offer the world in the various moral and economic crises it now faced. But Islam's new confidence and assertiveness sometimes led to harsh confrontations with the non-Muslim world around it.

Many of these conflicts stemmed from Muslim unease. Islamic economic and political gains were far from evenly distributed. Some nations, like Saudi Arabia and Kuwait, were rich, while others, like Bangladesh and some of the Muslim African states remained among the poorest on earth. Some Muslim governments, while independent, were corrupt and undemocratic. Some Muslims felt that, despite independence, the West still exercised far too much influence, both economic and cultural, in their societies.

Belief: The basic beliefs of Islam are expressed in a statement that all Muslims profess: "There is no God but God, and Muhammad is his Messenger (Rasul)."

Islam maintains that God is absolutely one, without a second, neither begetting nor begotten. Thus, it strongly rejects the Christian notion of the *Trinity.* Islam also maintains an absolute distinction between the creator and creation. To confuse creation and creator is to commit the fundamental sin of idolatry, that is, the association of other things with God. Muslims believe that Christians commit this sin when they claim that Jesus was God incarnate. So do people who place any goal above following the will of God, such as the pursuit of wealth.

Muslims believe that God has everywhere revealed himself to his creation in some form. They also believe that prophets in a line beginning with Adam and including such figures as Abraham, Moses, and Jesus have disclosed special revelations from God. Muslims call the communities that follow these revelations "People of the Book." But through the activity of Shaytan (more commonly known in North America as *Satan*), these revelations were misunderstood. With Muhammad, the line of God's prophets comes to a climax, and God's revelation to human beings is complete. This implies that the Qur'an is the complete and final manner in which God addresses human beings. And because God would not give his most sacred truth to just anyone, it also implies that Muhammad provides the model of how human beings should respond to God's revelation and implement justice in the world.

In addition, Muslims believe in Angels, one of whom, Shaytan or Iblis, rebelled against God, They also believe that there will be a final judgment at the end of time and that the faithful will enjoy an eternal existence in Paradise.

Practices: In discussing how Muslims practice their religion, it is customary to identify five "pillars" of Islam. All Muslims practice these pillars, although they differ over details.

The *first pillar is profession of the faith (shahadah)*. A Muslim cannot truly submit oneself to God's will without professing the divinity of God and the special place of the prophet Muhammad.

The *second pillar is obligatory prayer (salat)*. Muslims may pray at any time, but they are also enjoined to pray more formally five times a day. (Many Shi'ites incorporate these prayers into three daily prayers.) They face the town of Mecca (the compass direction varies depending on where in the world they happen to be), adopt several postures, and recite a series of prayers. Noon prayer on Fridays is, when possible, done as part of a congregation at a mosque. There an Imam also preaches a sermon to the assembled congregation.

The *third pillar of Islam is almsgiving (zakat)*, for the Prophet urged his followers to care for the poor and the needy. In Islamic countries almsgiving has generally been administered by the government. Private charity is also widely practiced.

The *fourth pillar is fasting during the ninth month of the Islamic calendar, the month of Ramadan (sawm)*. From sunup to sundown during that month, Muslims refrain from eating, drinking, and sexual activity. The fast recognizes significant events in the early history of Islam, such as the first revelations to the prophet Muhammad. It also teaches compassion for those for whom fasting must be a way of life. Those who are pregnant, sick, old, or traveling are not expected to fast. The month of fasting ends with a feast, the *Id al-fitr*.

The *fifth pillar of Islam is Pilgrimage to Mecca (hajj)*. This is a formal ritual that takes place during the final month of the Islamic year. Ideally, all Muslims should make pilgrimage once in their lives. But they may not do so if they are too sick to travel, if their absence would mean hardship at home, or if they incur economic hardship to do so. On the tenth day of the month, Muslims throughout the entire world *Sacrifice* a goat, sheep, or cow. Known as *Id al-Adha*, this feast commemorates the story of God commanding Abraham to sacrifice Ishmael (for Jews and Christians, Isaac).

The Islamic calendar is based on the cycles of the moon rather than on the solar year. As a result, over an extended period the Ramadan fast and pilgrimage to Mecca will have occurred in every season of the year. This also applies to *Ashura*, which Shi'ites observe on the tenth day of the first month, *Muharram*. It commemorates the death of Husayn, son of Ali and grandson of Muhammad, the third Shi'ite Imam, who lost his life in battle at Karbala (in Iraq) in 680 CE.

The five pillars do not appear as such in the Qur'an. They come from the *Hadith*. Some Muslims occasionally speak about *six pillars, adding Jihad* to the five above. Although jihad has come to be associated in North America with "holy war," it technically refers to the struggle against temptation. This struggle can involve warfare if one is called on to defend the faith in response to military aggression.

Organization: Sunni and Shi'ite Muslims differ over how the community should be organized. For Sunnis, political and religious leadership may be exercised by different persons. Traditionally, caliphs and sultans oversaw matters of internal order and external defense. Today different officers, namely, presidents and prime ministers, fulfill these functions. Religious authority resides with the *ulema*, scholars of Islam.

For Shi'ites, political and religious leadership are ideally exercised by the same person, the male descendant of Muhammad known as the Imam. A Shi'ite community known as the twelvers believes that the imam, last seen in 873 CE, is exercising authority while in hiding. Their religious leaders, headed by the Ayatollahs ("reflections of God"), are considerably more independent than their Sunni counterparts. Another Shi'ite community, known as the Nizari Ishailis, believe that the imam is still present in the world. Known as the *Aga Khan*, he exercises authority over a worldwide community.

Like some schools of Christianity, Islam has not traditionally recognized the ideals of separation of religion and government and of religious pluralism that have now become common in Europe, North America, and other parts of the world. Like other societies, contemporary Muslim societies are addressing the issues posed by the modern ideal of the secular state.

Significance: Since the time of the prophet Muhammad Islam has been one of the world's major religions. At the beginning of the 21st century roughly one-fifth of the world's population practiced it, including more than four and a half million North Americans. In addition, Islam has given the world rich cultural traditions, including art and architecture, literature and philosophy.

Religious Doctrine: The Quran – was written in Heaven, given to Muhammad by the Angel Gabriel as the word of Allah. Muhammad was proclaimed a Prophet.

Ideology: In Chapter 8, The Challenge, the author identifies many passages from the Quran that indicates violence. Because of that, there is a question as to whether it is a religion or a war machine.

Hinduism   *950 Million*

Hinduism is the predominant and indigenous religious tradition of South Asia.

Hinduism is often referred to as Sanatana Dharma (a Sanskrit phrase meaning "the eternal law."

Most forms of *Hinduism* are henotheistic religions. They recognize a single deity, and view other Gods and Goddesses as manifestations or aspects of that supreme God. Henotheistic and polytheistic religions have traditionally been among the world's most religiously tolerant faiths. However, until recently, a Hindu nationalistic political party controlled the government of India. The linkage of religion, the national government, and nationalism led to a degeneration of the separation of church and state in India. This, in turn, had decreased the level of religious tolerance in that country. The escalation of anti-Christian violence was one manifestation of this linkage. With the recent change in government, the level of violence may diminish.

Hinduism has grown to become the world's third largest religion, after Christianity and Islam. It claims about 950 million followers -- about 14%

of the world's population. It is the dominant religion in India, Nepal, and among the Tamils in Sri Lanka.

Belief: *Hinduism* differs from Christianity and other monotheistic religions in that it does *not* have a single founder, a specific theological system, a single concept of deity, a single holy text, a single system of morality, a central religious authority, or the concept of a prophet. Because of the wide variety of Hindu traditions, freedom of belief and practice are notable features of *Hinduism.*

Religious Doctrine: *Hinduism is* not a religion in the same sense as Christianity is; it is more like an all encompassing way of life -- much as Native American spirituality is. It is generally regarded as the world's oldest organized religion. It consists of "*thousands of different religious groups that have evolved in India since 1500 BCE.*"

Ideology: Hindus are peace loving people. Their doctrines and beliefs are pleasantly accepted by other religions of America.

Buddhism   376 Million

Buddhism currently has about 376 million followers and is generally listed as the world's fourth largest religion after Christianity, Islam *and* Hinduism. It was founded in Northern India by Siddhartha Gautama (circa 563 to 460 BCE).

Belief: Buddhism does not generally deny the truth of other religions; instead, it tries to supplement another truth with a truth of its own. As a result, Buddhists often worship the gods that their non-Buddhist neighbors worship. But in Buddhism it is ultimately more important to follow the Buddhist path than to worship gods.

One follows the Buddhist path to redress the root problem that all sentient or conscious beings face; suffering. Buddhism blames suffering, along with bondage, to the world of ordinary existence and rebirth (samsara) on ignorance. Two kinds of ignorance are most important. The first kind leads people to think and act as if they are eternal, unchanging selves or souls. The second leads people to think and act as if things persist, when, in fact, Buddhism teaches, absolutely nothing at all is eternal and unchanging. Ignorance of the truths of "no self" and "impermanence" leads to attachment and craving, and they in turn lead to suffering. To obtain release from suffering *(nirvana)* a person must overcome ignorance. That requires an intellectual acknowledgement of Buddhist truths, but it also requires much more. It requires a total transformation of one's thoughts, actions and experiences.

Organization: During the 45 years of his wandering as the Buddha, Siddhartha Gautama organized his community into two groups, the Sangha, that is, the community of monks and nuns, and the lay supporters. This organization has been typical of Theravada Buddhism. Monks and nuns beg for their food and devote their lives to following the Buddha's path. Political authorities such as kings and queens have always been important lay supporters.

Practices: Just as Buddhism has not required its adherents to reject other religious beliefs, so it has not required them to refrain from other religious practices. As a result, Buddhist practice varies widely. Japanese Buddhists participate in Shinto rituals. Buddhist in parts of Southeast Asia engage in spirit-cults.

Significance: Buddhism is one of the world's most important religions. At the end of the 20th century, it had more than 300 million adherents. Buddhism has profoundly influenced philosophy, literature, and the arts in Asia for over 2,000 years. In recent decades it has also been extremely popular in some segments of American society.

Ideology: The Buddha did not advocate the worship of any particular god. He did not deny that gods existed, but he thought that because gods are living beings, they, too, needed ultimately to escape from suffering. This religion is very friendly.

Judaism   *17 Million*

Judaism is the "religion, philosophy, and way of life" of the Jewish people Originating in the Hebrew Bible (also known as the Tanakh) and explored in later texts. The religion centered on the covenant revealed to Moses at Mount Sinai and preserved in the Torah, the first five books of the Hebrew Bible. Judaism is a major religion. In addition, both Christianity and Islam see themselves as continuing the ancient tradition of Judaism.

Belief: As a religion, Judaism is much more a way of life than a set of belief. The Talmud, for example, concentrates on what one needs to do in order to follow God's commandments, not on what one ought to believe.

Nevertheless, Jews have generally held several beliefs. These include the conviction that there is one, eternal, omniscient, incorporeal God who created the universe, that he alone deserves worship, and that he revealed the unchanging Torah to Moses as a guide to life.

Religious Doctrine: The Torah. The first five books of the Hebrew Bible, traditionally said to have been written by Moses, are known as the Torah. It is the story of the beginning.

Organization: Judaism is organized according to local congregations that join together to form national organizations. A congregation maintains a synagogue, which is a place for prayer, study and fellowship. It also supports the Rabbi, a person who, after intensive study, is ordained to serve a congregation's spiritual needs

Rabbis are generally respected for their learning and their service to the community.

The state of Israel, established after the Holocaust, has a special place in the Jewish World. Its political leaders have no religious authority, but by its constitution every Jew in the world may become an Israeli citizen. Most Jews outside the state strongly support the state.

Practices: The goal of Judaism is to make life holy, to grace the temporal with the eternal and the material with the spiritual. Jews do this by following God's commandments (mitzvot), so far as they can. These commandments are taken as a sign of God's love and concern. In Judaism God is like a compassionate parent.

Significance: At the end of the 20th century roughly 17 million people practiced Judaism. Although this is only a small percentage of the earth's population, Judaism remains a major religion. In addition, Judaism has enriched other religions of the world, such as Christianity and Islam, and individual Jews have made major contributions to the world's culture.

Ideology: The Jews are peace loving people.

Sikhism   16 Million

Belief: Every morning the Sikhs pray a Prayer known as the Japji. It summarizes Sikh teachings about God: He is one and true; He is the creator; He is present in all the universe but is not subject to the laws of rebirth.

Sikhs believe that God cannot be found in images. Instead, they find God in his name, in the ten Gurus, and in the Guru Granth. Sikhs believe that by following God's path people can become pure

Religious Doctrine: A religion from northwest India that traces itself back to 10 Gurus, beginning with Guru Nanak (1469-1539). Today the Sikhs venerate above all a book of writings known as the Adi Granth or Guru Granth Sahib.

History: Guru Nanak lived in the Punjab, 'the region of the five rivers' in northwest India. At the age of 30 he had an extraordinary religious experience. Afterward, he began to preach a distinct religious path that went beyond the differences between Hindus and Muslims. Nanak was followed in succession by nine other Gurus or Teachers. The fifth Guru, Arjun, began building the most sacred Shrine of the Sikhs, the Golden Temple of Amritsar in northwest India. He also collected writings from his predecessors into a book known as the Adi Granth.

From 1526 northern India was ruled by the Mughal dynasty. The Mughals were Muslims. At first relations between the Sikhs and the Mughals were good. But in 1605 Jahangir came to the throne. He tortured and executed Guru Arjun because he thought that Arjun had adulterated Islamic teachings. In response, the Sikhs saw themselves as called to be soldiers as well as saints. In the face of continuing persecution, the last guru, Guru Gobind Singh (1666-1708), established a Sikh community known as the Khalsa. He also ended the line of human Gurus and transferred his authority to the Adi Granth

In the 19th century the Sikhs decided British rulers were preferable to Muslim ones. Many Sikhs became soldiers in the British army. With the establishment of India and Pakistan in 1947 and 1948, some Sikhs began to agitate for the establishment of a separate Sikh state.

Practices: Sikhs worship together in a building known as a gurdwara. There the Guru Granth rests upon an elevated platform, where it is decorated with flowers and fanned. During worship, Sikhs listen to and participate in singing from the Guru Granth and receive a sweet in return. Sikh holidays include the birthdays of Guru Nanak and Guru Gobind Singh and the anniversary of the Guru Arjun's martyrdom.

Organization: Most Sikhs are members of the Khalsa. They observe what are known as the "five k's" (in the Punjabi language each stipulation refers to a word beginning with "k"): They do not cut their hair, including beards in the case of men; they carry combs; they wear special steel bracelets; they carry swords; and they wear a special kind of pants. Male Sikhs generally wear turbans over their hair.

Sikhism has no formally ordained priests, although certain sects recognize living gurus.

Significance: Once considered a sect of Hinduism, Sikhism has come to be recognized as a religion in its own right. At the beginning of the first century, it claimed roughly 20 million adherents.

Ideology: Sikhs are peace loving people.

Baha'iism   *5 Million*

A religion founded in Iran in the 19th century. The Baha'i faith sees itself called to unite spiritually all the peoples of the world.

History: During the 1840s a religious figure in Iran known as the Bab (Gateway) predicted the coming of "the one whom God shall reveal." In 1863, one of his followers, now known as Baha'ullah (1817-92) claimed to be that one.

The teachings of the Bab and of Baha'ullah threatened the authority of orthodox Islamic scholars. As a result, Baha'ullah spent much of his life in exile and in jail. From 1868 until his death he lived in what is now Israel. For that reason the center of the Baha'i community is located in Israel.

When Baha'ullah died, control of the community passed to his son, known in the Baha'i community as Abdal Baha (1844-1921), and his grandson, Shoghi Effendi (1899-1957). It then passed to a board known as the Council of the Hands of the Cause (1957-62) and finally to an elected assembly, the International House of Justice (1962-present).

Organization: The Baha'i faith sees itself continuing the revelation of God found in Judaism, Christianity, and Islam. The Prophets of each of these traditions, it teaches, were genuine messengers from God. Each of them fulfilled the task assigned by God. But Baha'is insists that the process of God's revelation will never end. Neither Moses, nor Jesus nor Muhammad was the last of God's messengers. For the contemporary world there is a new messenger, Baha'ullah. He was made known a new task: to unite spiritually all people.

Baha'is are enjoined to pray in private every day. In addition, local communities gather together on the first day of every month. (Baha'i months are 19 days long) A major Baha'i festival is Noruz, New Year's. In accordance with Persian practice it is celebrated on March 21, the time of the spring equinox. During the month prior to Noruz, Baha'is observe a fast. They neither eat nor drink from sunup to sundown; they eat and drink at night. (Muslims observe a similar fast during the month of Ramadan. Moreover, Baha'is are never permitted to drink alcohol.

Religious Doctrine: During the 20th century a leading initiative of the Baha'i community was the construction of major houses of worship, one on each continent. The design of each house of worship reflects significant elements of its location. For example, the house of worship in New Delhi, India, is in the form of a lotus, a sacred plant in India. The brick work of the house of worship in Panama reflects some work in the ancient temples of middle America. At the same time, all Baha'i houses of worship share certain features. For example, they have nine doorways and nine sided domes. Baha'is see the number 9 as a sign of the highest unity. Therefore, the doors and domes emphasize the unity that Baha'is believe characterizes God, all people and all religions.

Ideology: Because of its closeness to Islam and its origin in Iran, it is not certain if this religion is one of peace or radical, as is Islam.

Confucianism   5 Million

Confucianism is an influential East Asian spiritual and ethical tradition. It originated with Confucius at the end of the sixth century BCE. Since then, Confucianism has often been the official ideology of the Chinese state.

History: Confucius (Latin for Kung-fu-tsu, Master Kung, 551-479 BCE), was a profoundly influential teacher who emphasized that, because human beings are social creatures, a good society is important to a good human life. But he also realized that a good society, in turn, depends on good, highly motivated people. The first goal, then, was to cultivate humaneness within oneself. He believed this was something that all people can do. He is said moreover to have edited five classic books of Chinese thought, and his disciples gathered his own teaching into a collection known as the Analects.

Later Confucians taught proper behavior in terms of five relationships: ruler-subject, father-son, elder brother-younger brother, husband-wife, and friend-friend. They also developed specific views of humaneness. Mencius (Chinese, Meng-Tzu) (372 – 289 BCE) had an optimistic view of the human being. Humaneness, he said, is present in all human beings; it simply needs the right nurturing in order to blossom and flourish. Hsun Tzu (300 – 238 BCE) disagreed. In his view, people are nature evil and uncivil. To avoid the evils that result from greed and contention, people must be restrained by teaching and observances. At the time Hsun Tzu was more influential. As time passed, however, Mencius's positions came to dominate Confucian thinking.

Religious Doctrine: In 195 BCE, the Han emperor offered a pig, a sheep, and an ox at the grave of Confucius. This act marked the beginning of the official link between Confucianism and the Chinese government. To become a government official, one had to pass grueling examinations in Confucianism and the Confucian classics. The cult of Confucius also became a major part of an official's duties.

When the Han dynasty ended in 220 CE, Confucianism was temporarily eclipsed. Its place at court was taken by Buddhism and Taoism. But around 1000 CE the fortunes of Confucianism began to rise again. Important neo-Confucian thinkers like Chu His (1130 – 1200 CE) and Wang Yang-ming

(1472 – 1528) provided Confucianism what it had seemed so severely to lack: a metaphysics (thought about the nature of reality) as lofty as that of Buddhism and Taoism. Confucianism became the dominant ideology of China. It was also the senior partner in a religious union that included Taoism and Buddhism.

By the 19th century, Confucianism had become moribund. Many Chinese rejected it as old-fashioned and powerless, especially in contrast to the newly arrived European powers. The democratic revolution associated with Sun Yat Sen (1866-1925) and then especially the communist regime established by Mao-Tse Tung (1893 – 1976) cut the ties between Confucianism and the government. On the Mainland, Confucianism suffered severely during the Cultural Revolution of 1966 – 1969, but the Chinese state in Taiwan preserved Confucian rituals as part of its cultural heritage.

Teachings: Confucianism focuses on how human beings behave in society. It strives to identify the ideal way to live.

In Confucianism the ideal person is the noble person. For Confucius, nobility did not derive from birth. It derived from cultivating true humaneness (jen). This was done, Confucius believed, through the practice of Rituals (li). The rituals Confucius had in mind, however, were not religious rites. They were rituals of respect that one showed one's fellow human beings. One can begin to see how truly radical Confucius's teachings were. He redirected the focus of religious observance. The attention one used to give to the ancestor one now gave to life in this world.

The five relationships within which people cultivate virtue mentioned above are clearly not relationships between equals. They are also clearly male-centered. Indeed, some Confucians have suggested that since the relationship between a mother and her child is a natural one, the father-son relationship should be seen as the foundation of society. In any case, the relationships are not one-sided. Each person has responsibilities. For example, a younger brother should respect an older brother. But if the older brother wants respect, he should act only in ways that are worthy of respect

Practices: To practice Confucianism individual persons cultivate virtue by carefully performing their responsibilities. These include responsibilities that North Americans would call religious as well as those they would call ethical. For example, the philosopher Wang Yang-ming recommended sitting quietly as a way to cultivate spirituality.

The primary ritual of Confucianism, as the Chinese state religion, was Sacrifice. Confucians performed sacrifices for ancestors, especially the ancestors of the emperor, for those who first brought culture, and for Confucius himself. They also performed sacrifices for spirits associated with political institutions, for the powers of nature, and for the universe as a whole.

The elaborateness of a sacrifice depended upon how important the occasion was. On the most important occasions the sacrificial victims included a pig, a sheep, or an ox. In performing the sacrifice, either the emperor or a high official would bow, present the offerings, and pray. At the same time, Incense was burned and musicians would play.

Organization: No professional priests conducted the cult of Confucianism. Scholars trained in Confucian teachings did. This was one of their duties as officials of the Chinese state. When the emperor was present, he took the leading role.

A special government ministry was in charge of the state cult. Among other things, it provided the materials used in the sacrifice, established the proper procedures to be followed, and set the calendar, so that the rituals would be performed at the proper time.

Significance: Confucianism has defined the traditional values and ideas of proper behavior in China. Although it is out of favor in communist China, it lives on in Taiwan. Confucianism has also profoundly influenced traditional values and ways of life in Korea, Vietnam and Japan.

Ideology: This religion coexists well with the other religions.

Jainism   4 Million

A religion in India, Jains get their name because they follow the teachings and example of the jina, which means victor. For them, the victor is Mahavira (sixth century BCE) He discovered the way to conquer the forces that keep people bound to continuous rebirth, known as Sanskrit as Samsara.

Belief: Jains claim that their religion is millions of years old. For them, Mahavira is the 24th in a line of tirhanskaras or ford-makers. These are people who have made fords across the stream of samsara. At least in its present form Jainism grew from a broad movement in northeast India in the sixth century BCE. At that time sramanas – men and, to a lesser extent, women – gave up ordinary family life. They also rejected the sacrifices described in the sacred books known as the Veda. Instead, they wandered, begged for food, and devoted themselves to teachings and practices that promised spiritual liberation. The most famous religion to grow out of this movement is Buddhism. Jainism is another.

Buddhism is practiced all over the world, but Jainism remains confined to India. In the centuries after Mahavira, it spread along trade routes to southern and western India. These are its two strongholds today. In the first century CE, the community split. The cause was a dispute over what those who wander must give up. One group insisted that they must give up clothes entirely. Their community is called Digambara, "sky-clad." Another group insisted that it is enough if the wanderers wear only a simple white cloth. Their community is called Svetambara, "white-clad." Digambara Jains are particularly strong in the south Indian state of Karnataka. Svetambara Jains tend to live in the West Indian state of Gujarat.

Digambaras and Svetambaras have different sacred books, but they share the same basic beliefs. Like Hindus and Buddhists, Jains believe that people are continually reborn. This rebirth results from action (Sanskrit, Karma). Unlike Hindus and Buddhists, however, Jains say that a particularly fine kind of matter is involved in this process. Whenever the human life-force, the jiva, acts, this fine matter sticks to it and weighs it down. The goal of Jain practice is to cleanse the jiva of karmic matter. When the jiva is clean, it rises to the highest point in the universe. There it remains undisturbed forever.

Religious Doctrine: The Jain community has two unequal levels. Monks and Nuns adopt a lifestyle based on wandering and begging. Laymen and Laywomen maintain households and work. On both levels women are generally in an inferior position.

Monks and Nuns are said to be closer to ultimate liberation. A cardinal rule that governs their behavior is noninjury (Sanskrit, Ahimsa). Svetbara Monks and Nuns wear clothes over their mouths, sweep the paths where they walk, and strain their water to avoid harming little living beings. The most advanced Jains go even further: In old age they enter liberation by refraining from eating and drinking until they die.

Laymen and Laywomen follow ahimsa, but to a lesser extent. As a result, all Jains are strict vegetarians. Jains have also established several animal sanctuaries. In addition, laymen and laywomen give food and drink to monks and nuns – gifts that help them make spiritual progress. They also visit temples. There they worship before images of the tirhankaras. Jain temples include some of the most famous religious monuments in India: the lush marble temples at Mount Abu and some of the richly decorated temples at Khajuraho.

At the end of the 20th century there were only about four million Jains in the world. But in championing ahimsa and vegetarianism, Jainism has had a profound impact on Indian society. For example, it strongly influenced the leader of the Indian Independence movement, Mohandas Gandhi.

Ideology: Jainism is a peace loving religion.

Shintoism *3 Million*

Shintoism is a Japanese religion of the indigenous gods of the country. The word Shinto means "the way of the Gods." This is to distinguish it from the way of the Buddha, or Buddhism, the other great religious tradition of Japan.

Religious Doctrine: Shinto is the worship of the Kami, or ancient Japanese gods. Many of those worshipped now were there long before Buddhism arrived in Japan in the sixth century CE and are still honored in the Shinto shrines of Japan today.

History: In the Middle Ages kami and buddhas were often worshipped together. The kami were considered guardians of the buddhas, or sometimes special Japanese forms of the same spiritual power seen in Buddhism as a Buddha. But in modern times Shinto shrines and Buddhist temples have been kept separate. This is largely because the nationalistic governments that ruled Japan from 1868 up until the end of World War II in 1945 wanted to make Shinto a separate patriotic cult, untouched by anything of foreign origin like Buddhism. The extreme nationalists emphasized that the emperor of Japan was himself a kami and descended from Amaterasu, kami or goddess of the sun. He was therefore worthy of all honor and sacrifice.

However, Shinto as a religion is much more than an example of religious nationalism. The kami of most shrines are peaceful deities, protectors of families and local communities, honored in festivals that have their roots in the agricultural year. They were there long before the extreme nationalists, and have outlasted them. Though the emperor of Japan is still installed with very ancient Shinto rites, his religious and political role is now almost always seen as purely symbolic.

Beliefs and Practices: The visitor to present day Japan will see evidence of Slhinto on every hand. In most places one is not too far from a Shinto shrine or jinja, large or small. Large city shrines are on park like grounds, with grass and one or two old trees. In the countryside, shrines are often in places of striking natural beauty: on a mountainside, by a waterfall, beside the ocean or a lake or a rushing stream. Wherever situated, the entry to a Shinto shrine is marked by the distinctive gateway called a torii, which has become a symbol of Shinto as recognizable as the Christian cross or the Jewish Star of David. Passing under the torii, the visitor will approach the shrine itself, a small wooden building. In the front will be a sort of porch, perhaps containing such characteristic Shinto symbols as a drum beaten during sacred dance, gohei zigzag strips of paper fastened to an upright pole, and in the center a mirror indicating the presence of divinity. In a section behind the porch an eight-legged offering table may be seen. Behind it, steep steps lead up to massive closed doors. These doors, usually closed, open into the *honden* or inner sanctuary of the shrine, where a special token of the kami presence is kept.

Persons passing a shrine often pause to pray. They will come to the front of the shrine, clap their hands twice or pull a bell-rope, bow, and whisper a Prayer. Priests present offerings at shrines periodically. The great occasions of a shrine, however, are its annual *matsuri* or festivals. Then the shrine really comes to life. Festivals are planned and prepared for weeks, and usually draw large crowds. They have a happy, holiday atmosphere, but begin with solemn worship and prayer.

First the priests enter the shrine in their white or pastel robes and black *eboshi* or high rounded hats. The chief priest next purifies the shrine and the assembled crowd through a gesture like waving an evergreen branch. Then the offerings are slowly and carefully advanced and placed on the offering table. Offerings are usually beautifully arranged dishes of rice, seafood, fruit, vegetables, salt, water, and sake or rice wine. When they are all in order, the chief priest stand behind the table and chants a *norito* or prayer. Then the offerings are slowly removed.

After that, the *matsuri* changes to its festive mood, kept a little differently in each shrine according to local tradition. A carnival may open on the shrine grounds. Maidens may perform sacred dance. The kami may be carried vigorously through the streets in a palanquin called a *mikoshi*, borne on the shoulders of young men. Many shrine traditions are famous and draw spectators to the pageantry of their *matsuri* from afar. Celebrated attractions include grand parades, bonfires, horse or boat races, dances, and much else, all usually in colorful traditional costumes.

Significance: For many Japanese, Shinto is important because it provides links to the rich traditions of their nation's past. Spiritually, it emphasizes the importance of purity, for the kami and their shrines are thought to be very pure places, and one can purify one's own mind and heart by closeness to them. As a polytheistic religion, one affirming many gods and goddesses, Shinto suggests that the divine can be found in many different local forms, and by this means is close to the lives of communities and people.

Shinto Festivals: Celebrations held at Shinto shrines in Japan. The Japanese celebrate a great number of festivals, many of them connected with Shinto, the indigenous Japanese religion. Some are celebrated nationwide; others are festivals specially celebrated at a particular shrine.

As the ancient religion of Japan, Shinto has many connections with farming. Two very common Shinto festivals are the festival to pray for a good harvest, held in the spring, and the harvest festival, held in the fall. Shinto is also connected with growth on the human level, and some festivals celebrate the growth of children into adults. They include a festival on November 15, at which parents present at a shrine sons aged three and five and daughters aged three and seven; a festival for girls on March 3, a festival for boys on May 5, and a festival at which people who turned 20 years old in the preceding year visit a shrine on January 20.

Shinto festivals are both solemn rituals and joyous, even ribald affairs. At the shrine itself priests purify the sacred area; worshippers then bow, present offerings to the KAMI, pray, and entertain the *kami* with music and dance. Offerings include water, salt, sake (rice wine), vegetables and seafood products, but nothing that has blood, such as meat. Worshippers commune with the *kami* by drinking sake that has been presented at the shrine.

Festivals also resemble great fairs. It is very common to celebrate festivals with a procession in which several worshippers carry portable shrines for the *kami* in parades through the streets. Other common events at festivals include plays, sumo wrestling, and feasting. Some festivals have events that are peculiar to them. Examples include kite battles at the Hamamatsu Kite-Flying Festival (May 3 – 5), dances performed by unmarried women holding lilies for the Lily Festival at the Isakawa Shrine (June 17), and various forms of horse races at the Soma Wild Horse Chase Festival (July 23 – 25).

Ideology: This is a peace loving religion that poses no problem to the other religions of the world.

Zoroastrianism   *200,000*

Zoroastrianism is a religion begun in Iran by the prophet Zarathustra. Its followers worship only one God, Ahura Mazda. Zoroastrianism teaches that the world is the site of a struggle between good and evil. It also maintains that there will be a final judgment after death.

Beliefs: The sacred collection of writings of the Zoroastrians is known as the Avesta or Zend Avesta. Among other writings it contains hymns by Zarathustra known as *Gathas*. Because Zoroastrinism has suffered throughout its history, only part of the Avesta survives today.

The central figure of Zoroastrian worship is Ahura Mazda, also known as Ormazd. He is eternal and uncreated and is said to have seven heavenly attendants, led by Spenta Mainyu, sometimes translated as "Holy Spirit." Opposed to Ahura Mazda is Angra Mainyu, "Evil Spirit," also known as Ahriman.

Zoroastrians think of the world as a battle ground between these two sides. The heavenly attendants of Ahura Mazda have chosen to follow Truth. Angra Mainyu and the daevas have chosen to follow the Lie. Human beings are now called upon to choose Truth over the Lie, goodness over evil.

Religious Doctrine: Zoroastrians also teach that there will be a final battle at the end of time. In that battle Ahura Mazda will defeat Angra Mainyu once and for all. They also teach that human beings are judged after death. They must walk across the Bridge of Recompense, which traverses an abyss. For a deceased person who has followed the Truth, the Bridge is wide. He or she crosses easily and enters the presence of Ahura Mazda. But if the deceased has followed the Lie, the Bridge becomes as narrow as a razor's edge, and he or she falls into the abyss.

History: No one knows when Zarathustra lived. Some date him close to 1000 BCE. Others date him in the sixth century BCE. In any case, he lived in eastern Iran and reformed the traditional Iranian religion. He advocated the worship of Ahura Mazda (Lord of Wisdom) as the one true God. He also conceived of the traditional *daevas* – a word related to the English word "deity" – not as gods but as evil spirits. He eliminated the Sacrifices that the daevas originally received.

Zoroastrianism flourished under the Persian emperors known as the Archaemenids. The emperors Darius (ruled 522-486 BCE) and Xerxes (ruled 486-465 BCE) made it the official religion of their empire. The precise relations between Zoroastrianism and the traditional Persian priests known as Magi are disputed.

After the conquests of Alexander the Great (356-323 BCE), Zoroastrianism adopted a very low profile. Little was heard of it again until the Sassanids came to power in Persia (ruled, 224-636 CE). At that time, Ahura Mazda became known as Ormazd; the evil spirit opposing him became Ahriman. Several offshoots of Zoroastrianism also appeared. These included Manichaeism, a once prominent religion whose adherents were spread from the Atlantic coasts of Europe and North Africa all the way to the pacific coast of China.

Beginning about 635 CE, Muslim armies invaded and then conquered Persia. The vast majority of Persians converted to Islam. As a result, perhaps only 25,000 Zoroastrians, known as Gabars, remain in Iran today. They are concentrated in the remote cities of Yazd and Kerman.

By 1000 CE Zoroastrians from Persia began settling in the western Indian region of Gujarat. There they are known as Parsees, because they came from Persia. For centuries the Parsees practiced agriculture, but under British rule in the 19th century they entered business, education, and professions and became very influential. In the 19th century Parsees began to leave India and settle in trading outposts of the British Empire. In the period after Indian Independence in 1947 significant Parsee communities were established in London and Toronto.

Practices: The most common symbol of Zoroastrianism is fire, for Zoroastrians think that fire is supremely pure indeed. Zoroastrian temples are known as fire temples. They contain fires that burn continuously in large metal vessels. Five times a day priests tend the fires. They add fuel and recite prayers from the Avesta.

Observant Zoroastrians bathe ritually for purposes of purity. Their daily life is also divided into five different Prayer periods. The most important Zoroastrian festival is New Year's. Known as No Ruz or "New Day," it is a joyous celebration held around the time of the spring equinox.

At the age of seven for Parsees, 10 for Gabars, boys and girls become members of the community through a ritual known as *navjot*, "new birth." On this occasion they receive a white shirt and a sacred thread. They wear them for the rest of their lives.

The Zoroastrian practice best known to outsiders is probably the funeral, although it is simply one facet of a rich religious life. Zoroastrians believe that it is wrong to pollute any of the four elements, earth, air, fire, or water. Therefore, they have traditionally not buried or cremated their dead. Instead, they have placed the corpses in specially constructed wells known as "towers of silence." Relatively quickly, vultures eat the fleshy parts of the corpse. The bones are then dried by the sun and gathered into special holding areas or ossuaries.

In recent decades this practice has been the subject of some discussion with 'Zoroastrian communities. Those who live in areas where there is not a large concentration of Zoroastrians find it difficult to maintain the tradition. Some bury the dead. Others advocate electric cremation as a viable alternative to exposure.

Organization: One can be a Zoroastrian only if one's father is a Zoroastrian. The community does not accept converts. Parsees say that they had to agree not to accept converts in order to gain permission to live in India.

A man may become a priest if his father was a priest. He receives special instruction, traditionally from his father. He also undergoes special Rituals to invest him with the office of the priesthood.

Significance: the number of Zoroastrians in the world is not large, perhaps 200,000. Nevertheless, Zoroastrianism is a major and ancient religion. In addition, significant elements of Judaism, Christianity, and Islam may be of Zoroastrian origin. These elements include beliefs in Angels, in the devil, in a final judgment, and in a Resurrection of the dead.

Ideology: Zoroastrians are peace loving people.

Taoism   *100,000*

A Chinese religion: pronounced with an initial "d," and therefore also spelled Daoism. Taoism teaches that by living in harmony with the Tao (pronounced and sometimes spelled Dao) or the way of nature, it is possible to prolong life and even become immortal.

Scholars have often distinguished two different trends in Taoism: philosophical Taoism and religious Taoism. Philosophical Taoism refers to ideas put forth roughly from 600 to 200 BCE. Religious Taoism refers to movements and practices like Alchemy (transforming metals into medicines that were thought to grant immortality) and Meditation that began around the first century CE. These two trends help to distinguish two major stages in the history of Taoism. But it would be incorrect to think that philosophical and religious Taoism was entirely separate movements.

Belief: The earliest Taoist texts celebrate the Tao. According to the beginning of the Tao Te Ching, it is impossible really to give the Tao a name. It is simply indescribable. At the same time, the Tao is the mother of all things. It produces everything in the world, including ourselves.

Religious Doctrine: The founder of Taoism is known as Lao-Tzu, "Old Master." He may have lived in the sixth century BCE, or he may be only legendary. It is said that Lao-Tzu dictated the classic book of Taoism, the Tao Te Ching, as he was leaving China in old age. In any case, by the fourth century BCE a book in 5,000 Chinese characters had come into existence that advocated yielding to the way of nature in all things. It called the prime characteristic of that way *wu-wei*, action that lacks deliberate intention. A later book developed these insights further. It was named Chuang-Tzu after the person who supposedly wrote it.

History: In the first century CE several movements used these figures and books to develop rituals and institutions. Some looked for a golden age to come in the future. This age was known as the great peace. Those who followed Taoist principles were expected to rule during that peace. Inspired by such teachings, many secret movements tried to usher in the golden age. Among them was an attempt to overthrow the Han dynasty in 184 CE.

Another Taoist movement that began in the same period is known as "the way of the heavenly masters." Its founder claimed to have received revelations from Lao-Tzu, whom he considered to be a god. Among other things, the movement promised to heal the sick. It also provided its members with a series of books or "registers" in which to record their spiritual progress.

The first millennium (1-1000) CE was the golden age of Taoism. Taoists developed elaborate Rituals. They also perfected many techniques that were said to lead to long life and, if done just right, immortality. Occasionally Taoism became the official religion. Different kingdoms required their subjects to perform Taoist practices, for example, to celebrate the birthday of Lao-Tzu.

The first millennium CE was also the time when Buddhism came to China. Taoists often opposed Buddhism, and they convinced several rulers to outlaw it. The two religious did, however, influence one another. Taoist ideas helped transform Buddhism. This can be seen especially in the school known in China as Ch'an and in Japan as Zen Buddhism. Perhaps under Buddhist influence, Taoists developed monasteries and convents funded by the state.

Throughout most of the second millennium (1001-2000) CE Confucianism dominated official Chinese religion. The official outlook promoted the unity of the three religions, Confucianism, Taoism, and Buddhism. During this period Taoism developed forms more suited to the needs of private individuals than of the official cult.

With the victory of communism in mainland China in 1949, and especially the Cultural Revolution of the late 1960s. Taoism suffered tremendously. Because the government objected to both old traditions and religion, it opposed Taoism. In the 1980s some Taoist institutions were rebuilt and

Taoist worship resumed. Meanwhile, Taoist practice flourished in Chinese communities elsewhere especially on Taiwan.

Teachings: The earliest texts advocate that human beings should live in harmony with the Tao. Consider, for example, water flowing in a stream. What does it do? Strictly speaking, it does nothing. It simply yields to the forces exerted on it. It falls because of the force of gravity; it moves out of the way when it hits a boulder. Yet in simply yielding, water proves to be stronger than the boulder. It wears the boulder away. Taoists find this example instructive. The human action, they say, is action that is not forced by deliberate intention. The earliest Taoist texts also apply these ideas to government. That government is best whose subjects are hardly aware of the government's activities at all.

Later Taoism develops a full range of mythological ideas. It teaches that there are many immortals. Some immortals are connected with the world at large. Others are connected with the human body. Taoism has other teachings, too: about islands of the immortals in the eastern ocean, where elixirs of immortality may be found; about the five sacred mountains in China, the most sacred of which is T'ai Shan in the eastern province of Shantung; and about the life-giving properties of various substances, such as gold. In addition, Taoism analyzes the human being in detail. For Taoism, the most important life-force is the original breath known as *chi*. Chi and other life-forces concentrate in three centers: the head, the heart, and the navel. These three "fields" are where the three "holy ones," the three most important immortals, dwell. They are also home to three beings known as "worms" that devour the vital energy and bring about death.

Practices: There are two main kinds of Taoist practice: exercises to prolong one's life and large, elaborate rituals for the well-being of the community.

The exercises to prolong life try to preserve or restore the vital energy with which a person is born. Certain practices, called the "external elixir," involve eating and drinking, especially the eating and drinking of metals. For the ancient Chinese, gold symbolized the state that all Taoists sought. It could neither be destroyed nor corrupted. The "external elixir" attempted to synthesize gold from baser substances, especially lead and mercuric sulfide (cinnabar). In theory one acquired long life either by using vessels made with synthesized gold or eating and drinking it. These practices are the source of what came to be known in Europe and North America as alchemy.

Around 1000 CE the "external elixir" was replaced by an "internal elixir."

In these practices Taoists do not eat or drink physical substances. They perform rituals instead. The rituals include meditation and breathing and gymnastic exercises.

Like the two "elixirs," the great public rituals, known as *jiao*, provide long life to the priests who perform them. They also give peace, health, and protection to the community as a whole. In these colorful festivals, the three "holy ones" are invited to a feast. Technically, only the Taoist priest offers the feast, but member of the community also participate with rituals of their own.

Organization: Taoism has had both Monks and Nuns. But the number of nuns has always been extremely small and the majority of Taoist priests are not monks but live in families.

In Taiwan today there are two orders of priests. Those with red headbands perform only rituals of Exorcism. Those with black headbands also perform the major public festivals.

Some Taoist communities, such as "the way of the heavenly masters," have been carefully structured. Today the head of the community, sometimes called a pope, still claims to be a descendant of the original founder. At times Taoists have also formed secret societies dedicated to the overthrow of the Chinese government.

Significance: In addition to its immense contribution to Chinese society, Taoism attracted the attention of Europeans and North Americans in the 20th century. Ideas from the early Taoist texts became popular. So did physical exercises such as T'ai Chi and Taoist-influenced martial arts

Ideology: Except for the secret societies dedicated to the overthrow of the Chinese government, this is a peace loving religion.

SUMMARY

In the original version of this chapter, it was called "Creating A Religion – Would I Be A Prophet?" The point was, if I chose Noah as the lead character, and we could develop enough of a following – like Islam in the early stages - would it make me a Prophet?

I was not trying to discredit Muhammad. In spite of the Quran's insistence that it was written by Allah, I think not. However, I think that Muhammad did a remarkable job of creating the illusion of grandeur in assembling the Quran.

We know that the last 9 chapters were added after his death. So, the fact is, not all of the Quran could have been written by Allah. I'm saying that none of it was because of the threats and redundancy throughout the Quran.

Christianity, (*Belief that Jesus was the Son of God, preached and performed miracles);*
Islam *(Mecca to Medina by Muhammad in Arabia - 622CE);*
Hinduism *(Indus Valley Religion of India - 3500-1500 BCE);*
Buddhism *(Siddhartha Gautama in Tibet – 560-480 BCE);*
Judaism *(Moses on Mt Sinai, Abraham in Israel 1800 BCE);*
Sikhism *(Guru Nanak in northwest India - 1469-1539 CE);*
Baha'iism *(Iran Bab "gateway" predicted the One to Come – Baha'ullah, in 1840);*
Confucianism(*Kung-tu-tzu in China – sixth century BCE);*
Jainism *(Jina of India – 6th century BCE - ford makers);*
Shintoism *(Japanese, "way of the Gods" worship Kami – 6th cen BCE);*
Zoroastrianism *(Prophet Zarathustra of Iran – 6th century BCE*
Taoism *(Chinese religion Lao Tzu "Old Master" 4th century BCE "the way of nature in things").*

At the end of each religion is a sub-title – *Ideology*. The ideologies of all the religions of the world are basically calm, reverent and non-violent. Taoism has an underlying attack on China, but overall, they, too, are calm and preach love and peace. This is not true with Islam.

Islam, through the Quran, spews hatred of the Infidels, the non-Believers, and suggests killing them.

Does that sound like a Religion? In the chapters ahead, it gets worse.

The next Summary is on page 78.

Chapter 5

Minorities and Racial Difficulties

Overview

I have seen an astounding number of Black men and women dressed in Muslim attire. Therefore, I thought it would be appropriate to introduce this subject here to explain the rapid growth of Islam in America.

I have spent a fair amount of time in the south; initially during the 50s while the south was still segregated. It was a rude awakening for me; coming from Hawaii, one of the world's first melting pots, then into the south, where the racial divide was established.

Knowing what I have learned about Islam, there is a parallel in lifestyles that is worth discussing to see if we can reach a conclusion as to where and how the Muslim faith can flourish, or fail, in America.

Unity

To unite the races, it has to start from the top. As long as the members of Congress and the Senate insist on having a Black Caucus, racial unity can never happen.

(Barack Obama was voted into office to deal with correcting the racial problems in our country, and, to date, all he did was make it worse. Now, every spoken word is taken out of context and turned into a racial issue. And, no one has figured out whether he does that on purpose or not)

Add to that audacity; the Black History month *(when there's no White History month)* or true history as recorded in school books of old before the Department of Education decided to re-write history, Kwanza *(for the elitists who wish to have their own Christmas),* Quotas and people who claim to be Black Leaders spouting off whenever a Negro gets into trouble with the law or for whatever reason.

When the Whites get into trouble, there is not a spokesperson that makes an issue of it. That's the way it's supposed to be.

Why is it that no one is disturbed with the NAACP, and yet Blacks are offended being referred to as *"Coloreds?"* or *"Negroes?"* Also, the phrase *"persons of color"* should be avoided. I'm a person of color – more color than many Negroes. Does that make me a Negro?

Instead of trying to accent his racial status, if a Negro could count his blessings because his ancestors were selected and sold into slavery, brought to America, paid the price so that when the slave owners learned of their faults and they *(the slaves)* were set free, the Negro could rejoice that he is a free man in the greatest country on earth *(thanks to his ancestors)*, instead of being in the country of his ancestors who are still living in less than pleasant conditions in Africa.

If everyone could rejoice in freedom, we would be on our way to unity. I won't see that in my lifetime, but it's a beautiful thought. I would have to be President for that to happen.

Back To The South

I have witnessed, first hand, the racial divide of segregation that was established in the south.

I have lived through the atrocities of racial indifferences in the south long before this generation of Blacks and Whites, and know the solutions, but was never in a position to do anything about it.

I was in Phenix City, Alabama when it was the hot spot of racial turmoil. I have watched the riots caused by the assassination of Martin Luther King, Malcom X's issues, the King beating issue in California and the riots caused by the OJ Simpson trial and many others.

It was always interesting to see the Black leaders take to the airwaves in defense of the racial issue, which to me, just added fuel to the fire. The Black leaders seemed to need some "face time in the media" to be assured of recognition as a Black Leader. It was appalling that when the tide was turned with a White person as the victim, that the same Black Leaders were nowhere to be found.

My Black Friends And Relatives

When World War II was declared over, the troops from the Pacific Theatre who were engaged in combat in the islands surrounding Japan, Iwo Jima, and other points in the Pacific, were returning to America.

Many sailed from various ports and stopped over in Hawaii before heading for Oakland CA.

Hawaii welcomed the troops home parading them through the streets of Honolulu and on the main street in Waikiki, Kalakaua Avenue.

The excitement level was high for the troops and for the civilian populace, as well. It was more than most of the troops could handle, as they broke ranks from the parade to hug the many beautiful ladies along the roadside, who were cheering them for a job well done.

Merchants were offering the troops merchandise and food items. There were lei vendors who were getting bombarded with requests for flowers and leis for the troops. There was dancing in the streets. The bars were overrun and emptied into the streets which turned into a Mardi Gras before New Orleans thought about it.

Nine months later, the Baby Boom overwhelmed Hawaii. My little brother was in that mix. There were many mixed breeds that came out of all that celebration, and some of the handsomest guys and prettiest gals grew up in the customs of Hawaii and made the islands a more beautiful place to visit and hail from.

The half Blacks that emerged from the celebration, however, weren't exactly happy with their fate. It is great growing up in Hawaii because it is such a melting pot. The camaraderie is uniquely different being a Polynesian – so much customs, heritage and Koko *(blood)*.

I have had an opportunity to talk with many who were friends, as well as, relatives who shared their experiences in the military towns who were looked down upon as part of America's low class. I lived their grief myself and sympathized. But, they were all glad to come home to Hawaii where it has always been Home and the love never ceases to flow.

It's too bad that Hawaii consists of only eight little islands. Otherwise, I would recommend that all the Blacks of America go to Hawaii and forget about the racial strife that they had to endure for so long. It is my goal to package the "Aloha" from Hawaii and spread it throughout America.

Close Black Friends

I have many Black friends. My neighbor is a classic, rarity. He's a conservative, an Army veteran and a retired educator. His wife is a pretty and lovely gal from Jamaica.

We lived in the neighborhood for about six months before we had a chance to meet. They were there a couple years before we decided to move into the neighborhood. What great people. They would do anything for us. And, we would return the favor ten-fold for the friendship that they blessed us with.

One of the Black guys who worked with my wife at the Firm was a former homeless, drug addict that was at the end of his rope before God told him how disappointed He was in him. Jon pulled himself together and started working as a lawn caretaker, graduated to Landscaping and then collected old clothing from his clients to give to the homeless.

A little here and a littler there, Jon was able to clean himself up and got a job with a real company before moving up to the Firm of which he holds a responsible position. And, even with his busy schedule, he still finds time to collect old clothing from friends and former clients who still remember him, especially around Christmas time.

Jon is a big guy. He's fairer than I am. About five years ago, he married an adorable Black gal who didn't have children. Jon was already fifty and his wife close behind. They looked into the possibility of adoption and got lucky with a boy and a girl, brother and sister, who were dark and left with an agency.

Jon has become such a close brother that he shares all his wonders of parenthood with me and I am always so glad that everything was working out so well for him.

One day, Jon was changing his shirt to take the children hiking. The boy looked at Jon's bare body and said, "Dad, you're White!" Jon laughed and couldn't wait to tell me about that. I will see Jon and his wife at the Firm's Christmas party this year.

Jon has a Christian group of friends who would get together to pray for those who are grieving for whatever reason. And, whenever a tragedy occurs that affect people within the firm, you can count on seeing Jon leading a worship service, like an in-house minister. You've got to love this guy.

Through the years with veterans' organizations, I have bonded with many Blacks because we share experiences of the horrors of combat. These friends, like Jon, bare their life stories with me because I have been a trusted brother, of sorts. Whenever I have questions regarding racial incidents that appear in the news, I can discuss issues openly with my band of brothers.

Black Muslims

I have seen many Black females dressed in traditional mid-eastern riff complete with veils covering their faces. And, naturally, the first question that goes through my mind is; 'Is it so bad to be a Black in America that these women would want everyone to think that they are mid-Easterners, rather than Black?'

When I see a Black female with her children dressed as Muslims, I would question the motive of the mother. Did she agree with her husband to become a Muslim knowing that she is thought of as a second rate citizen in the culture of Islam? Or, is it better to be a Muslim, than a Black? Or, better still, how could she do this to her children?

I was tempted to inquire of these ladies the reasons for their conversion to Islam, but they looked so bad - as in ugly - that I just assumed that the Blacks didn't want anything to do with them. Maybe, that's why they converted to Islam.

I know a couple Black men who have become Muslims. I had to ask them what exactly motivated them to convert to Islam. What I learned from them was what I expected. They were disturbed with the racial issues of America and found closeness in Islam when they were introduced by a friend into the faith. They didn't question the faith because they received the blessings from their sponsor in prayer.

This is a frightening issue. How easily minorities, especially Blacks, are preyed on and the growth of Islam marches on.

Blacks appear to be the focal point of Islam to convert America into a Muslim country. By my personal observations and calculations, they are succeeding very well.

The disturbing part is – Why would Blacks want to become a Muslim if they knew that it was the Muslims (Islam) back in the 16th Century that sold their ancestors into slavery? That was the beginning of the slave trade. You might want to read Dr. Peter Hammond's books on the slave trade.

A Ruling Class

Islam has set their sights on Minorities and the disadvantaged as an easy target to help develop their base here in America. Currently, the population of Muslims stands at just over ten million and growing at an alarming rate.

Think about your problems in a racially divided America. Would converting to Islam help you and your situation? Could you bridge the gap in the racial divide by converting to Islam? But, most of all, when you learn about their doctrine, will you feel blessed or torn apart by your decision? Be an American while you can. The world is changing, and not necessarily in your favor, unless you're thinking of becoming a radical to get even with America. That would be a crying shame.

The Problem

If the Black Leaders spent more time talking about solutions, rather than blaming the Whites for the problems, America would have had their racial differences solved. Kumbaya would be in effect.

Let's take a look at what I'm talking about – starting with Hawaii.

When I was growing up, it was not "Cool" to be a Hawaiian.

About sixty years earlier, the Hawaiian Islands were hit with a plague, Hawaii did not know of any diseases. When the common cold was introduced by the influx of foreigners, the immune system of the Hawaiian people were not able to combat it. The people were dropping dead by the hundreds.

The labor force was affected. The King *(of Hawaii)* had to request help from the Emperors of Japan and China to send people to help as a temporary labor force in the pineapple and the sugar cane fields.

The numbers of Whites and Asians, who were responding to the requests for help by the King, grew so rapidly that the foreigners outnumbered the natives quickly. The Hawaiians who survived the plague soon became second-rate citizens because they did not contribute enough to the work force.

The influx of people was fine. The work force conducted their tasks in harmony with each other. But, it turned out that the bosses were White.

And, as is normal, the dark-skinned people were usually considered the lowly. So, the problem mounts into a racial issue.

Perception

It didn't take long for the Asians and Polynesians to learn that the way to overcome the prejudices was to perform their work ethics in such a way that the Whites could not complain or direct negative remarks at them.

As a matter of fact, the outstanding performance of assigned jobs was such, that all the people were praising the Asians and dark-skinned natives for it.

Let me add a historical event. During World War II, the 442nd Combat Team that was organized in Hawaii, consisting wholly of Hawaiians and Asians, became the most decorated and outstanding combat unit of the war.

Today, as I walk the streets of Hawaii, or anywhere for that matter, there is a pride that goes with the dark-skin. And, as I walk, the pride of being part Asian, part Hispanic as well as Hawaiian, walks with me. That pride started by work ethics of my parents and the way they taught me and my siblings, and it trickled down through the generations.

The Asians and Hispanics have proven themselves as hard-working and focused people in everything they do. Sure, there are always exceptions, but those are few as compared to the multitude of successes.

Fast Forward

To the Blacks of America, instead of bashing the White man for bringing slavery to America, which is not correct, consider this: Where would you be, today, if your ancestors didn't come to America as a slave? Would you still be in Africa? Is that where you want to be now?

Even with the economy being as bad as it is right now, you are still a lot better off in America than you could possibly be living in Africa. However, if you disagree with me, would you move to Africa if you were offered Free Travel?

Advancing Past Slavery

It's been over a hundred years since slavery came to an end in America. Yet, many Blacks are still stuck on Slavery. They're having difficulty getting off the mistreatment of their ancestors.

Many Black parents are not allowing their children to grow up being disciplined, kind and caring Americans. They're ensuring that the children never forget that their ancestors were tormented by the White man.

There's nothing wrong with remembering your roots, but do it in a positive way; glory in the freedom that you have to choose to be whoever and whatever you wish to be in the greatest country in the world.

Those same parents are always caught up in racial issues reported by the media and are easily misled by their so-called Black Leaders who take to the airwaves proclaiming racism and mistreatment on a Black reported incident.

Just last week, I was sitting in a meeting discussing incidents that took place in a Black neighborhood. One of the Black guys who work with the court system told us that there is a generation of Black youths who do not know about common decency because they grew up in 'Crack' houses with a void of parental guidance.

The neighborhoods are scary places to be if you're not from the 'Hood.' Step out of line if you are asked about your purpose for being there may well cause bullets to fly. The picture painted by many of the Blacks in the group was not a good one. Color it 'Scary.'

So, faced with the absence of a generation lacking discipline and half of the remaining Black populace unhappy about their fate as 'Blacks in America,' what would be the best course of action to take to get everyone on the same page? *(I hope – Not Islam)*

Look At The Positives

You're enjoying freedom, I hope. Think of all the people in the world who are not free to do what they want to. Many of them, supposedly free, are shackled by Liberalism, Socialism and even Communism and Slavery in some cultures *(Islam, as an example)*.

Think about your ancestors. How would they respond to the freedom now enjoyed by you and everyone in America? Would they feel proud that they were instrumental in bringing this change and this new lifestyle for Blacks?

Put yourselves in their shoes, but wake up to freedom today. Do you think that you would marvel at the freedom you have to do anything you want to do?

Take it another step. The Blacks today are being treated so well, the Whites are being slighted in many instances. But, forget the Whites for a moment.

If I were a Black man today, I would boast being a descendant of a Slave. I would want all the people in America to know my heritage; that of being a descendant of a Slave. Why would I do that, you ask? I would do it because I would be proud of being a Born Free American.

I would be proud to walk next to my friends, regardless of race *(color or creed)* and flaunt my heritage, if asked, of the price my ancestors paid for my freedom in America.

I would be bursting with joy as a Free American, rather than a questionably free person in any other part of the world.

I would band with other Blacks who feel the same way that I do about the racial divide and join forces with the Whites and be proud to be an American.

The N Word

Why would anyone call you a Nigger? Is it because you are being one?

In order for us to move ahead, we've got to get past these little quirks that were created by someone who had nothing else to do but make trouble.

Frankly, I think that everyone ought to be able to call each other by any name he feels like calling him. If you are offended by it, change your image so that you're not called by that name anymore.

Growing up in Hawaii, I learned that all the different people used to call each other by some mean names: Japs, Yobos, Potchos, Bodinkis, Pakpaks, Buddha head, Chinks Chinaman, Katonks, Podogees, Kanakas, Pilaus, Papaas, Buk Buks, Paeles, Haoles, Hu pe, *(I hope I didn't forget anyone),*

The people knew that they were obviously performing in a way that was less than acceptable to the name caller. They adjusted their performance to be in keeping with the accepted standard. And, Hawaii emerged the best, peaceful, loving melting pot of the world.

It is so crass, lacking in discrimination and sensibility, that we try to dodge the issue by creating the "N" Word. So, if no one can call you by that name, does it make you any different?

I remember as a little boy when I was called a Kanaka. I knew it was said to hurt me. It was said offensively. So, I had to tell my mother about the incident. Her response to me was: 'Were you acting like one?'

And, I thought to myself; 'You're supposed to be on my side.' Then, she said, 'Don't tell your father that!' I knew what she meant. I also knew that my Dad would get all over me for being anything but kind and respectable. Dad was so good with words. I wished he would just spank me and get it over with.

Come to Hawaii. Meet the people. Grasp the way they coexist with each other in the islands. Learn what causes the people to really love and care for each other. When you figure it out, you will be on to the secret of the islanders. They are like siblings. They hate each other, but try and pick on one of them and you'll have your hands full. *You know what I mean.* Then, go to your home and spread the Aloha that you got from Paradise and be yourself.

What Are They Saying About You

I know all the things that Blacks say about the Whites. But, here are a few things that the Whites say about the Blacks.

In a sentence, they say that Blacks are: Arrogant, Rude, Unkind, Disrespectful, Loud and have bad attitudes. Blacks are always in a hurry, can't wait in line, they have to get in the front, buck the line if they have to, but drag their butts across streets slowing traffic, they always crowd in the front of the bus – no one is in the back, they won't let a White person be in front of them, and usually park their vehicles illegally.

When I first came to the South in the 50s, none of what the Whites are saying today was true. Blacks were kind, caring, calm, loving and helpful. It wasn't until 1958, at the end of segregation, that the attitudes of the Blacks changed.

With their newly earned freedoms, many sought to be identified as Leaders to lead the masses. For the most part, they misled the masses in what has become the racial divide in America.

So, how do we bridge the divide? To me, the answer is a simple one – pretend you are a White, or an Asian. Get past the racial divide. Be as kind, caring, calm, loving and helpful as your grandparents, or great grandparents, were in the 50s.

Ask them about the old times – there were a lot of bad times that will tear them up, but the many good times will bring tears of joy.

One more thing; don't forget to *Smile*. A *Smile* is contagious A *Smile* projects warmth and caring. A *Smile*, if sincere, disarms your guest and demands a positive response. A *Smile* should be your guiding star as you move into your new world.

Proud To Be White
- Michael Richards

You can Google this article Proud To Be White by Michael Richards.

Michael Richards, better known as Kramer in the series "Seinfeld" had performances of his own where he supposedly made racial slurs and was charged with such. In his defense, he presented his case by example after example of how Blacks create different programs, but if the Whites did the same thing, they would be considered Racist.

His court presentation should be a "must read" for everyone.

Hope

Be American. Be Free. Be Black and Be Proud.

When Barack Hussein Obama became the first Black President of America, although I didn't vote for him, there was a degree of comfort of the change he would bring to our country that has been long overdue.

I envisioned him becoming one of the greatest Presidents this country has ever seen just by bringing the racial divide to an end and unite the people of our great country once and for all.

In the quest of greatness, I also envisioned him taking on the economic slump that he inherited, to turn the economy around and quickly be accelerated to heights unknown – far beyond Presidents Lincoln or Roosevelt.

I felt that his success was imminent. All he had to do was to slash taxes and to create an incentive for small business owners to boost their businesses; and for the large companies he could create a plan to entice the companies to bring their people *(businesses)* back to America and re-focus America as a booming economy and put America back to work.

Well, as I write my story, it's late 2010, and the Republicans have taken the House of Representatives back from a Democrat power base of both Houses.

How did it happen? How did the Democrats fall out of grace with their constituents? The answer is written in the winds.

In two short years, the President guided his power base into Health care reform and a Socialist agenda of Redistribution of Wealth. There were other plans that were brilliantly slid into place while the Republicans were distracted by chaotic trivia.

The Tea Party was formed. America was angry. They took to the streets to tell their Senators and Congressmen that they were not happy with the health plan that was being passed by votes paid for by the President and his leaders of both Houses with monies that would have to be repaid by the people, possibly by their grandchildren, and against their will.

The key words are: "against their will."

The Tea Party was successful in their objective to change the course of governance. Their many key figures spearheading the charge were a joy to watch. Among them were Former Alaska Governor and Vice-Presidential candidate, Sarah Palin, and Congresswoman Michelle Bachman. They restored pride and dignity, badly needed, to make the rest of the world know that our loss of sanity during our last election was only temporary.

I trust that the new Congress will hold firm to the resounding support of the people. Just by stopping the runaway spending and keeping the Bush tax cuts current, would improve our money base. That being the case, President Obama can take credit for an improved economy and the restoration of our monetary system, as was the case of the 1994 Congress.

The Problem Is Still There

Sadly, to correct it, it has to start from the top.

As I mentioned earlier, our Government is structured with a Black

Caucus. Why can't the problem be solved without resorting to a racial divide?

Who created Black History Month? Or, the Black Miss America Contest? Or Kwanza? The big hope, Barack Obama, to rid America of this racial divide that we anticipated didn't materialize. He failed us by trying to create a Socialist America so that the destitute, mostly Black, his voting base, would be cared for, indefinitely, at the risk of losing the Producers of America's monetary base.

Also, he tried to preserve his power base by creating a whole new generation of people dependent on the government for their well-being. He extended unemployment benefits to make the unemployed dependent on him and his party for support, just to get a vote or two.

Once An Angel

In my autobiography, I wrote about an incident involving a dear friend, a Black guy, and I want to share that story with you.

I am a member of a Gathering of combat veterans. We get together weekly. I noticed that one of the guys, a dear friend, had missed being there for four consecutive weeks. I thought to myself, 'I've got to give him a call to see if he's okay, or if he needs help – like somebody to talk to.'

That evening, while my wife and I were having dinner, I asked her to excuse me because I wanted to make a phone call. She asked: 'Could the call wait until after dinner?' I told her I needed to do it now because I would probably forget later.

When I dialed the number, it rang four times before the answering machine came on. So, I left this message:

> *'Willie, this is your big brother, Buddy. We've been missing you at the Gathering, brother. I just wanted to call to see if you're okay, or if you need help doing anything. Don't do anything crazy! We love you, Guy! Hopefully, we'll see you next week. Call me if you need help, Okay? Take care, brother.'*

Willie came to the Gathering the next week. He told me and the guys that he was sitting at the kitchen table when the phone rang.

He was so distraught with his life that he was going to end it all. He had the pistol in his mouth when the phone rang.

He stopped to listen to the message. When I hung up the phone, he

72

put the pistol down and cried. He mumbled to himself, 'I love you, too, brother.'

He thought about calling me back, but was so overcome by the true meaning of brotherly love, the band of brothers looking after each other.

When I told that story to my wife, she sobbed. She said, 'God called on you to be His angel. He couldn't have picked a better angel.'

With that comment, I teared.

Story Of An Angel

I have a friend, Phil, who grew up with me in Grade School who I recently spent five days in a Mini-Reunion with many of our classmates in Las Vegas. He is a veteran, and has had a lot of setbacks in life, overcame them, prospered, then became a very religious person. He sends me a lot of things via email.

Phil sent me this story which was so appropriate, especially since we're coming upon the Christmas season, that I thought I'd share it with you.

It was written by a Metro Denver Hospice Physician: (I could not reach him to get permission to use his story. You can Google it.)

Anyway, he was driving home from a meeting that evening about 5, stuck in traffic on Colorado Blvd., and the car started to choke and sputter and die – He barely managed to coast, cursing, into a gas station, glad only that he would not be blocking traffic and would have a somewhat warm spot to wait for the tow truck. It wouldn't even turn over.

Before he could make the call, he saw a woman walking out of the quickie mart building, and it looked like she slipped on some ice and fell into a gas pump, so he got out to see if she was okay.

When he got there, it looked more like she had been overcome by sobs than that she had fallen; she was a young woman who looked really haggard with dark circles under her eyes. She dropped something as he helped her up, and he picked it up to give it to her. It was a nickel.

At that moment, everything came into focus for him: the crying woman, the ancient Suburban crammed full of stuff with 3 kids in the back (1 in a car seat), and the gas pump reading $4.95.

He asked her if she was okay and if she needed help, and she just kept saying 'I don't want my kids to see me crying! So they stood on the other side of the pump from her car. She said she was driving to California and that things were very hard for her right now. So he asked, 'And you were praying?' That made her back away from him a little, but he assured her he was not a crazy person and said, 'He heard you, and He sent me.'

He took out his card and swiped it through the card reader on the pump so she could fill up her car completely, and while it was fueling, he walked to the next door McDonald's and bought 2 big bags of food, some gift certificates for more, and a big cup of coffee. She gave the food to the kids in the car, who attacked it like wolves, and they stood by the pump eating fries and talking a little.

She told him her name, and that she lived in Kansas City. Her boyfriend left 2 months ago and she had not been able to make ends meet. She knew she wouldn't have money to pay rent Jan. 1, and finally, in desperation, had called her parents, with whom she had not spoken in about 5 years. They lived in California and said she could come live with them and try to get on her feet there.

So she packed up everything she owned in the car. She told the kids they were going to California for Christmas, but not that they were going to live there. He gave her his gloves, a little hug and said a quick prayer with her for safety on the road. As he was walking over to his car, she said, 'So, are you like an angel or something?'

This definitely made him cry. He said, 'Sweetie, at this time of year angels are really busy, so sometimes God uses regular people.'

He said it was so incredible to be a part of someone else's miracle. And of course, you guessed it, when he got in his car it started right away and got him home with no problem. He'll put it in the shop tomorrow to check, but he suspects the mechanic won't find anything wrong.

Sometimes the angels fly close enough to you that you can hear the flutter of their wings.

Psalms 55:22 'Cast thy burden upon the Lord, and He shall sustain thee. He shall never suffer the righteous to be moved.'

'Father, I ask You to bless my children, grandchildren, friends, relatives and *email buddies reading this right now. Show them a new revelation of your love and power. Holy Spirit, I ask You to minister to their spirit this very moment. Where there is pain, give them Your peace and mercy. Where there is self doubt, release a renewed confidence through Your grace, In Jesus' precious name. Amen.'* Amen and Amen

This story really touched me, especially the prayer that Phil added to the end. I thought I would share it with you.

Be An Angel

When my wife mentioned God picking me as an angel, I recalled a number of times in combat and after when I reacted to different calls for help. I took risks and surfaced a hero in the eyes of those I helped.

I knocked on wood and thanked God for looking after me. But, was it me that was taking the risks, or was it God? Did He use me as an Angel back then?

Did God ever call on you to do something that you thought was crazy? Then you did it and discovered that some dear friend or relative was helped because of what you did?

Think about it. Were you ever called upon to be an angel?

Since my wife suggested that "God couldn't have picked a better Angel," my mind races into my past, in combat, at different crazy things that I did. And, I ask myself; 'Did He call on me then?'

If you were ever called on to be an angel, thank God for the opportunity to assist Him with his endless tasks. Because if He asked you to help Him, you know He is asking somebody, somewhere, to help you.

I don't want to get too mushy here, but think about it. I honestly believe that if you can identify with a time when you were asked to be an Angel, it will open a whole new world for you.

Helping others will become second-nature. Helping the Black Cause will be a blessing.

Helping America to Not Be Overcome By Islam will make you Very, Very Special. You would be an Angel just by being you and helping others. Amen.

The Warrior Prince

I was where you are right now. Imagine for a minute if the White man did not come to Hawaii, I may well have been a Prince.

Through the years, I have agonized over the changed hands of ownership of my homeland. I have vented by writing my story.

I have come to recognize that the "Big Guns" that helped the King (Kamehameha) to unite the people of the islands came from the White Man (America). And, when the foreigners introduced diseases to the islands that killed half of the population, the King had to ask the rulers of Asian countries to send help (labor force) that made the Hawaiians a minority in their own land.

Forgive? Yes! And, Accept! But, maybe, I will make a difference. That's what you're going to have to do.

The End of Racism

I have been on both sides of the issue. Whites confide in me because my wife is a pretty, radiant, influential and a trusted White girl. The Blacks confide in me because I understand their plight and I can share experiences they never thought of doing.

During my grandparents' era, they knew what it would take to turn the tide. They hunkered down and worked their buns off just for a little recognition that, sometimes, didn't come. But, the thing that did take place was the perception of high spirit and trustworthiness.

During that same era, your grandparents were overcome with joy and celebration of what should have been the end of racism. But, it turned out to be the beginning of a new racial divide when the new leaders tried to take credit for something that they did not do – it was given them by MLK and God.

What the Blacks are faced with now is an uphill battle because a couple generations went by where the people were crying the blues and were catered to in the name of Civil Rights. The Black Leaders who managed to be voted into the power base did little to help the Blacks. They were too busy taking care of Watash.

So, my recommendation of overcoming what the President failed to do is going to be a very simple task.

If I were President, I would end this racial divide. We've been banging our heads against the wall generation after generation and the problem is still there. Why? I don't think it's going to take a Black man or a Minority to end this divide. All it's going to take is RESOLVE. Get past the arguments and protests and learn to live with it.

Those who did not convert to Islam, but cannot or will not accept the policy can choose the country of their choice and can qualify for a Free Trip to that country.

End of Argument!

If You Think The Tea Party Is A Racist Group, You Are Still A Racist

Be American or Be Gone.

All In Favor Say, "Aye!"
AYE!

(LISTEN TO THE "AYES" RESONATING

ALL ACROSS THE COUNTRY.)

SUMMARY

This is a chapter worth reading. So, when you get through speed-reading your way through the book, please come back to this chapter.

Islam is preying on minorities to leave their culture and to join Islam who promise them *(minorities and disadvantaged)* a better life with better treatment, better recognition and acceptance with prayer partners who can assure them a place in Paradise.

We have to watch the down-trodden to ensure that they don't fall prey to Islam. How can we promise them a better 'life after death?' We have to preach the truth, as we know it.

In this chapter, I share experiences I had in the south, back in the '50s when it was still segregated. That was a rude awakening for me. I talk about the many times that I was mistaken as a Black and the harsh actions I took to overcome that.

Growing up in Hawaii, there were a lot of similarities of the way we were mistreated by the Whites. So, the comparisons I make are close to the heart. And, from them, I can say that Racism in America has gone on too long.

It has been over a hundred years since slavery came to an end, yet we are still stuck on slavery. It's about time that we end it and move on to bigger issues, rather than spinning our wheels on the Black Leaders who need "face time" on TV. This chapter spells out my plan.

Islam will indoctrinate the new members by telling them that Islam is the only religion and that by being faithful to Allah, they will be promised a place in Paradise when they pass from this life, and that their life after will be better than their life here on earth.

With all the promises of Paradise and a better life after death, it's no wonder that the Arabs have no problems in recruiting Suicide Bombers.

We have to get the truth out to discourage the under-privileged youths from volunteering to be Suicide Bombers so that they can go to Paradise and to be waited on by dark-eyed virgins, as suggested by the Quran.

The next Summary is on page 94.

Chapter 6
Origin Of Terrorism

Introduction

Just when I thought I had all the information that I needed to make my case against Islam, an ugly head pops up from the library of endless knowledge called Wahhabism which makes my "Challenge to Islam" even stronger.

9-11

Since the September 11, 2001, terrorist attacks on the World Trade Center and the Pentagon, there remains a great deal of mystery as to the source of the hatred that motivated nineteen Middle Eastern terrorist to conduct a Kamakaze act taking their own lives as they set out to kill thousands of innocent people?

Now that we know more about the terrorists – their stated mission, their organizational affiliations, some of their financial backing – the key question remains a puzzle: What larger forces drove them to undertake the most heinous terrorist attack in America's history? Can the source of their hatred be identified, to include their chain of command, so that it can be studied to understand and counter terrorist acts?

Since fifteen of the nineteen terrorists, as well as their leader, Osama bin Laden, were born and raised in Saudi Arabia, it was a fair assumption that Saudi Arabia's role as an ally was presumptuous, at best.

Saudi Arabia was established in 1932 by King Abdul Aziz (known in America as ibn Saud). Saudi Arabia has been economically aligned with U.S. oil interests.

But, September 11 has forced America to reassess Saudi Arabia's reliability as an ally. Analysts have leaked information to the Pentagon's

Defense Policy Board that Saudi Arabia was active at every level of the terror chain.

Wahhabism

Wahhabi Islam remains the dominant religious creed in Saudi Arabia. Many regard Wahhabism as a radical and violent departure from the mainstream Islamic tradition.

The founder of Wahhabism, Muhammad ibn Abdul Wahhab, was born around 1700 in the village of Uyaina on the Najd plateau in east central Arabia. This region of Arabia differed from the Hijaz, where the holy cities of Mecca and Medina and the cosmopolitan Red Sea port of Jeddah were located, and from al-Hasa, along the Persian Gulf coast.

Wahhab studied with his father, the *qadi* (religious judge) of Uyaina, then he moved to Medina, where he came under the influence of Hanbali Islamic scholars, admirers of the writings of the 14th century scholar Ibn Taymiyya (died 1328).

Ibn Taymiyya believed that foreign influence had seeped into Islam after the Mongol invasions of the Middle East. He denounced Muslims who had adopted Christian practices and objected to the veneration of Jerusalem, since such practice was borrowed from Judaism. Abdul Wahhab found Taymiyya's works so gripping that he actually copied them in his own hand.

Wahhab traveled outside of Arabia to what is today Iraq and Syria. There is evidence that he studied in the Persian cities of Isfahan and Qum during the reign of Nadir Shah (1736-47), who tried forcibly to return Persia to the mainstream branch of Islam, Sunni (orthodox path), after it had adopted Shiite Islam as a state religion in the early sixteenth century.

Wahhab became an exponent of Sufism, the mystical movement of Islam, but would eventually repudiate it. He also visited Basra in southern Iraq but was expelled because of his strong religious views. Having traveled throughout the main centers of the Muslim world, he was fully acquainted with the major schools of Islamic practice.

The Islamic world during this period was changing because the military expansion of Islam had stopped after the armies of the Ottoman Empire were blocked at the gates of Vienna in 1683. By 1771, the Ottomans would be ceding land to the Russians for the first time. British and Dutch ships were sailing into the Persian Gulf, establishing a commercial presence, as the Portuguese had a century earlier.

Returning to Arabia, Wahhab concluded that the Islam practiced throughout the Ottoman and Persian cities he had visited had been corrupted by foreign influences. The armies of Islam had seized many earlier civilizations but in the process had absorbed many of their practices. The veneration of saints, for example, including pilgrimage and prayer rites at their tombs, had become widespread.

Wahhab may have been trying to explain the rising power of the Christian West, which he claimed changed Islam under the Ottoman Empire. He developed his own unique approach to Islam, one that stressed the need to eradicate the differences from traditional Islamic doctrine, especially practices that leaned toward polytheism. He sought to restore the puritanical Islam of the Prophet Muhammad, and the early caliphs (al-salaf al-salibin). Years later, his followers would call themselves salafis. But in general, his movement was better defined by what it opposed than by what it advocated.

In his Book of Tawhid, Wahhab wrote, "We must find out what true Islam is: it is above all a rejection of all gods except God, a refusal to allow others to share in that worship which is due to God alone. Shirk is evil, no matter what the object, whether it be "king or prophet, or saint or tree or tomb."

The war against shirk (polytheism) became his central preoccupation. He was focused on what he claimed to be pure Islam, for the Quran states, "Kill those who ascribe partners to God, wheresoever ye find them." Polytheists (mushrikun) were his declared enemy – but his definition of polytheism was far different from that of the rest of the Islamic world.

In the name of his new strict monotheism, Wahhab destroyed the tombs of the companions, or first disciples, of the Prophet Muhammad, which had become objects of veneration. He demolished the tomb of Zayd bin al-Khattab, the brother of the second caliph of Islam, Umar bin al-Khattab. Prayer at tombs imitated Christian saint veneration.

But Christian influences were not his only concern. Just after its birth, Islam became between the mainstream Sunni branch and the Shiite branch. Initially, the two branches fought about who should be the Prophet Muhammad's successor (khalifah, or caliph). Sunni Islam soon won out; by modern times, only 16 percent of Muslims belonged to one of the various Shiite groups. During Wahhab's time, large groups of Shiites were in what is today Iran, Iraq, and Bahrain, and along the eastern coast of the Arabian peninsula.

The Shiites, who were the "partisans of Ali," Muhammad's son-in-law, added a theological lineage to the succession debate. They attributed special religious qualities to Ali and his sons, Hasan and Hussein, as well as to their descendants. Ali and his successors established an imamate, a hereditary dynasty, of spiritual leaders who possessed secret knowledge and miraculous powers; the twelfth imam is expected to return as a *mahdi*, or messianic savior, an intermediary between man and God.

Radicalism. Tribal raiding could now be carried on as a religious cause. What had been once taken as tribal booty was now demanded as *zakat* (the charitable payments required as one of the five pillars of Islam). Wahhab legitimized jihad against fellow Muslims for the first time. And, thanks to his military alliance with ibn Saud, he could duplicate the Muslim conquests of the seventh century.

One of the central doctrines of Wahhabism was takfir; a charge that Muslims could become infidels, or worse, by engaging in improper religious activities. Even a person who uttered the proclamation of Islamic faith, the *shahada*, but still practiced polytheism should be "denounced as an infidel and killed."

The Wahhabis were brutal to their enemies. To captured "polytheists" the Wahhabis offered a choice, embracing Wahhabism or death.

An independent revival of Wahhabism emerged in the Saudi-controlled Najd. This revival would prove vital to the new Saudi military drive.

After the September 11 attacks, some investigators have looked at the possible supporting role of Saudi Arabia. After all, a third of the prisoners the U.S. held from the war against bin Laden's al-Qaeda organization were Saudi nationals, as of the summer 2002.

One might protest that the Kingdom of Saudi Arabia is supposed to be an American ally, not a sponsor of international terrorism like Libya or Syria.

Ideology: The tendency in America is to not deal fully with the ideological basis of terrorism. We don't have to look any further than the terrorist organizations themselves to understand the centrality of ideology. An al-Qaeda training found in Great Britain outlines the necessary qualifications for any new member: the first qualification is a commitment to Islam, the second a "Commitment to the Organization's Ideology."

What do bin Laden and his operatives take to be Islam? According to at least one militant religious leader in Saudi Arabia, it is Wahhabi Islam that has provided the foundation for bin Laden's vast terrorist network.

In a book written after September 11, "Osama bin Laden is a natural continuation from Muhammad ibn Abdul Wahhab.

How has Saudi Wahhabism fostered the ideology of hatred that spawned suicidal terrorism? This question is inevitably linked to the question of how Wahhabism has treated the Islamic concept of jihad (literally, "struggle," but commonly translated as "holy war").

According to Islamic tradition, a warrior who gives his life in a true jihad, a holy war, becomes a *shahid*, or martyr (literally, "witness"), and is guaranteed entry into Paradise. The Wahhhabis restored the idea of jihad as armed struggle, and they spread their new doctrine across the Arabian peninsula and beyond in the latter part of the eighteenth century.

Analysts are uncomfortable investigating Wahhabism as a particularly radical form of Islam, especially given our tradition of Freedom of Religion. It is difficult for U.S. scholars of Islam to take a critical approach to a particular offshoot of Islam, even a radical minority sect, because it might be misconstrued as an attack on an entire religious tradition. Religious viewpoints are considered sacrosanct and therefore beyond scrutiny. Yet, U.S. analysts must delve into the mainstream Islam, so as not to make Islam, as a whole, into a new enemy.

Then, there is the factor of the Arab-Israeli conflict. Often, policy-makers suffer from short-sightedness when looking at the underlying reasons for problems in the Mideast; they focus exclusively on this conflict, and have become riveted to the Palestinian issue in particular. So, disproportionate diplomatic energy is invested in Israeli-Palestinian diplomacy at the expense of addressing larger regional issues, such as the 1979 Iranian revolution or Saddam Hussein's threats to Kuwait in 1990. It came as a surprise to us because we were stuck on the details of Arab-Israeli diplomacy.

Our focus on the Palestinian issue is based on the assumption that resolving this conflict would solve many other problems in the Middle-East – from obtaining basing rights for our Air Force in the Arabian peninsula, to forming an effective coalition against Iraq or Afghanistan, to achieving oil price stability.

This mistaken tendency has influenced the debate over the sources of contemporary terrorism. The British foreign secretary told an Iranian newspaper, "One of the factors that helps breed terror is the anger which many people in this region feel at events over the years in Palestine." A reporter of the Washington Post put it even more directly: "If we want to avoid creating more terrorists, we must end the Israeli-Palestinian conflict quickly." After September 11 came a slew of articles on the same theme.

Arab analysts have been more intellectually honest on this point; they tend to be among the first to point out that Osama bin Laden was not motivated by the Palestinian issue. His focus was on Afghanistan and on

Chechnya. In 1998, bin Laden spoke about a "crusader-Zionist alliance," his priorities were first Arabia, second Iraq, and third Jerusalem. Something else was motivating bin Laden and his supporters – something more fundamental than antipathy to Israel.

Ikhwan. A descendant of Wahhab, Abdullah bin Abdul Latif, who was the *qadi* (religious judge) of Riyadh, promoted a new religious movement that settled the area of al-Artawiya, a village in the Najd north of Riyadh.

Najdi settlers established the Ikhwan – a Wahhabi organization that insisted its "brethren" live according to strict Wahhabi ideology, avoid contact with Europeans, and reside in communal agricultural settlements known as *hujar* (*hijra*, in the singular).

The *hijra* movement spread through Arabia; some 52 settlements had been erected by 1920, and 120 by 1929. The Bedouin residents of the *hujar* continued to engage in military raids – but not just to plunder caravans, as they had in the past. Raiding in the Wahhabi tradition had a religious dimension; it entailed wars against the "polytheists."

In late 1915 Ibn Saud found that Ikhwanism was definitely gaining control of affairs in Najd. He saw that he had to make a decision: either to be a temporal ruler and crush Ikhwanism, or to become the spiritual head of this new Wahhabism. Probably in the first place he had thought to make use of it to strengthen his position, but in the end he was compelled to accept its doctrines and become its leader, lest he should go under himself.

Since the Ikhwan often came from Bedouin backgrounds and usually had not had extensive training in Islam, they tended to exhibit zealotry, if not fanaticism, in applying their newly found religion to their everyday lives. They beat fellow Ikhwan who did not pray five times a day, and regarded other Muslims as polytheists. The Ikhwan also wore distinctive clothing, including white turbans, instead of the traditional Arab *kufiya (roped headcloth)*. They covered their faces when they encountered Europeans or Arabs from outside Saudi Arabia, rather than allow themselves to be "defiled."

They brought this religious extremism to warfare, much as 18th century Wahhabis had done. In 1916, Ibn Saud issued an order by which all Bedouin tribes of Arabia had to join the Ikhwan and pay him *zakat*, the charitable donations required in Islam, because he was to be recognized as their imam. If they failed to make this payment, they faced conquest.

The Ikhwan viewed those who did not join them as polytheists – to whom they were utterly brutal. One Soviet historian called the Ikhwan the "white terror" of Arabia. They became instrumental in ibn Saud's subsequent conquests, inspiring Arabian tribes to join the cause.

Money and Oil - Saudi Power The British government had given Ibn Saud about 60,000 pounds sterling per year for the purpose of payments to the Bedouin tribes. In the early 1920s, the British subsidy was raised to 100,000 pounds sterling per year.

But, holding his enlarged kingdom together became an increasingly expensive proposition. He supported them with houses, food, cars, wives, and money. And he faced continuing military expenses.

From his control of Mecca, he benefited from the *Hajj*. But the number of pilgrims to Mecca declined from 130,000 in 1926 to 40,000 in 1931, and accordingly, *hajj* revenue fell by two-thirds. British officials told their American counterparts that the kingdom was "practically bankrupt." A strained national budget meant fewer subsidies for the bedouin – and fewer subsidies meant more difficulty holding the desert kingdom together.

In 1933, Ibn Saud granted Standard Oil of California (SOCAL) a huge oil concession covering 360,000 square miles in the eastern portion of the Saudi kingdom. Saudi oil royalties reached $10 million in 1946, and grew to $212 million by 1952. After the Second World War, CASOC took on two additional partners: Standard Oil of New Jersey and Standard Oil of New York. The expanded subsidiary changed its name to the Arabian American Oil Company (ARAMCO).

The Saudis had been schooled in the rules of the British Empire. Early in the century, the British had tied access to oil to their military strength as an imperial power. British oil companies like Anglo-Persian and the IPC were even partly owned by the British government. The United States, in contrast, wanted a straight business arrangement with no imperial trappings – it wanted American oil companies to be able to operate freely in Saudi Arabia, not any new formal security commitments. The American oil companies that owned ARAMCO were private firms; the US government was not a shareholder.

Though Ibn Saud was looking for something that the United States was not prepared to deliver – a formal defense treaty – Washington agreed to step up its military presence in Saudi Arabia. President Harry Truman sent a letter to Ibn Saud on October 31, 1950, reaffirming "US interest in the preservation of the independence and territorial integrity of Saudi Arabia."

A New Era Ibn Saud died in 1953. He had fathered forty-five sons from twenty-two different wives. The new king was his second son, Saud; His fourth son, Faisal, became the new crown prince.

King Saud struggled to hold together his father's legacy. He terminated the American air base at Dhahran in 1962, sought to placate Arab radicalism in the late 1950s, and plunged his country's finances into disarray. It would take until the 1960s, and the leadership of a new and more self-confident Saudi leader, for the influence of Wahhabism to be felt again on the international scene.

Saudi Arabia returned to its Wahhabi roots in 1964 when the third Saudi king, Faisal bin Abdul Aziz, assumed the throne after King Saud, his older brother, was deposed.

Faisal's mother was a direct descendant of Wahhabism's eighteenth-century founder, Muhammad ibn Abdul Wahhab. She died when Faisal was just six years old, in 1912, so the prince was raised in the home of his maternal grandfather who was a major Wahhabi scholar who had been Ibn Saud's childhood tutor.

The Muslim World League In 1952, Gamal Abdel Nasser, rose to power as Eqypt's president. From his 1956 confrontation with England, France and Israel over the Suez Canal, he became the unchallenged leader of Arab nationalism.

The forces supporting Nasser seemed ascendant as new Arab military regimes toppled the older Arab monarchies.

The Egyptian threat was not just external. Some Saudis rallied behind the Nasserism cause. The Saudi government had uncovered a pro-Nasserist plot within the Saudi armed forces. There was a global dimension to this struggle as well.

Even before he became king, Faisal turned to Islam as a counterweight to Nasser's Arab socialism. The struggle between the two leaders became an Arab cold war. The Saudis sponsored an international Islamic conference in Mecca in 1962 to devise a new Islamic strategy. At the conference's close, 111 *Ulama* and religious dignitaries established the Muslim World League, an international organization dedicated to the spread of Islam. They would revive Saudi Wahhabism and spread it globally.

The Muslim World League was effective in promoting Islam – and Wahhabism, in particular. The organization sent religious missionaries around the world, raised money to build mosques, and distributed the works of Muhammad ibn Abdul Wahhab. This led one specialist on modern Islam to argue that the Muslim World League was an effort to Wahhabize Islam worldwide.

Over the years, the Saudi leadership only consolidated its control of the Muslim World League. Some of the organization's secretaries-general became ministers in the Saudi government.

In 1963, King Faisal gave the Wahhabi religious leaders control over Saudi education. Of all the moves to install the Wahhabis in the seat of power, this decision would have the most far-reaching consequences.

The entire generation that was born during the 1960s and came of age during the 1980s grew up on Wahhabi doctrines. Despite the *ulama's* special responsibility for university education, the Education Ministry as a whole became a stronghold of religiously conservative bureaucrats. The Saudi government also installed backers of the Muslim Brotherhood at all levels of education. The curriculum used in schools focused on Islamic and Arabic studies, helping to preserve the grip of Wahhabism on Saudi society.

The Oil Weapon Originally, Faisal's instincts on the oil issue had been the same as his father's; Ibn Saud had been unwilling to put Saudi Arabia's American oil connection at risk as part of his support for the Arab states' war with Israel. Although Faisal had briefly suspended oil supplies to the United States and Great Britain after the Six-Day War, he still believed that oil should not be used as a political weapon.

Saudi behavior in the 1973 Yom Kippur War indicated that something fundamental had changed. One could argue that Saudi Arabia did not get involved in 1948 and 1967 because in both instances Israel was fighting the Saudis' greatest adversary: first Hashemite Transjordan, and then Nasserist Egypt. In fact, British diplomats in Saudi Arabia raised such a possibility when analyzing the 1948 conflict: "Even Saudi Arabia's hostility to Israel seemed in practice to be to some extent subordinated to her Hasemite complex, since Israeli strength might be a useful counterweight to Jordan."

Such an analysis might be even more relevant for the 1967 conflict, for the Israeli victory in the 1967 Six-Day War forced the Egyptians to withdraw their expeditionary army from Yemen, effectively terminating the Nasserist threat to the Arabian peninsula. By 1973, Nasser was gone, replaced by Anwar Sadat, and the Egyptian threat to Saudi Arabia was over.

That is when the Saudis backed Egypt, instituting an oil embargo against the United States – an embargo they lifted in the spring of 1974, after Egypt (and Syria) had reached a separation-of-forces agreement with Israel. Saudi oil had served Egyptian interests.

Muslim Brotherhood

The struggle between Saudi Pan-Islamism and Nasserism had other side effects that lasted for decades, even after Nasser's death in 1970. The most significant anti-Nasserist force in the 1950s was the Muslim Brotherhood, the organization that the Egyptian born schoolteacher, Hasan al-Banna (1906-49) had founded in 1928 in order to create a completely different political and social order as Egypt emerged from foreign domination – a society based on Islamic law. By this point, the Muslim Brotherhood had grown into a formidable political opposition in Egypt; as of 1949, the organization had two thousand branches throughout the country. But more significant, it was now a dangerous militant movement with a "secret apparatus" that acquired arms and terrorized its enemies.

In December 1948, a member of the Muslim Brotherhood murdered an Egyptian prime minister. Hasan al-Banna was assassinated less than two months later. In October 1954, a Muslim Brother made an attempt on Nasser's life.

Many Egyptian members of the Muslim Brotherhood who had been driven out of Egypt by Nasser's regime found refuge in Saudi Arabia, and some received stipends from the Saudi government. Palestinian Muslim Brothers followed. One of the founders of the Fatah movement had been a member of the Muslim Brotherhood. He left Egyptian-controlled Gaza to teach in Saudi Arabia. Yasser Arafat, who, though not formally a Muslim Brother, had fought as a sympathizer with their units in 1948.

Militant Jihad Sayyid Qutb, a prolific writer and thinker whose works included a six-volume commentary on the Quran, had argued that Egyptians were living in a modern state of spiritual darkness, or *jabilia*. Qutb claimed that Egypt had moved from the Dar al-Islam ("House of Islam") to the Dar al-Harb ("House of War"). The Arab regimes, he said, could legitimately become the object of a jihad.

Qutb predicted that eventually there would be a clash of civilizations between Islam and America, and that because America is morally bankrupt, it would crumble. Islam would assume the mantle of world leadership. Muslims, he said, had forgotten their own superiority, and thus jihad, an injunction of the Quran, had fallen into disuse. He renewed the call for a militant jihad: "He who understands the nature of this religion (Islam) will understand the need for the activist push of Islam as a jihad of the sword alongside a jihad of education."

Qutb reminded readers of their new militant mission: "A handful of men, with faith, troubled the impotent British empire at the Canal. They did not need heavy arms for that. If we regain our disciplined faith, we shall as did the early Muslims, defeat the great empires of the world. We can hold the balance between the great power of East and West."

In the 1980s, the Saudis welcomed Ayman al-Zawahiri, despite his past involvement in Islamic radicalism and in the assassination of Anwar Sadat (for which he had served a jail sentence in Egypt). In 1986, al-Zawahiri left Saudi Arabia for Afghanistan; in the late 1990s, he would become Osama bin Laden's deputy and al-Qaeda's chief ideologue.

But, most significant, Abdullah Azzam, one of the most influential Islamic fundamentalist thinkers, sought refuge in Saudi Arabia. It is difficult to overstate the impact that this Islamic radical had. His most important contribution to the Islamic fundamentalist movement was to restore the centrality of the idea of jihad.

Analyzing the reasons for the relative decline of the Islamic world, he reached a clear conclusion: "Anybody who looks into the state of Muslims today will find that their great misfortune is their abandonment of *Jihad.*"

In a famous Islamic legal opinion about defending Muslim land that comes under attack, he wrote, "In this condition the pious predecessors, those who succeeded them the scholars of the four Islamic schools of thought are agreed that in all Islamic ages, Jihad becomes obligatory upon all Muslims." And in a booklet entitled *Defending the Land of the Muslims Is Each Man's Most Important Duty*, he clearly made the jihad a new Muslim priority.

Wahhabism's Global Reach

Under the reign of King Fahd, Saudi Arabia extended its religious influence globally. Part of this expansion resulted from Fahd's need to bolster his religious credentials, given his reputation for gambling on the French Riviera and enjoying the good life in his many palaces in Europe. His palace in Marbella, Spain, had a hundred rooms; he owned a $50 million yacht; and his Boeing 747 was fitted with chandeliers, an elevator, gold bathroom fixtures, and a sauna.

The Taliban Saudi Arabia's initial Afghan links were driven by religious considerations as much as by its strategic interest in defeating the Soviet Union. The Saudis provided approximately $4 billion in aid to the Afghan guerrilla groups from 1980 through 1990 – excluding the grants given by Islamic charities and through the private funds of princes. In the early 1980s, the Saudis had two primary Afghan partners. One was Abdul Rasul Sayyaf, an Afghan Islamic scholar who had lived many years in Saudi

Arabia. He was sent to Peshawar, the Pakistani frontier town near the Khyber Pass into Afghanistan, in order to promote Wahabbism among the Afghan refugees. He actually set up a Wahhabi party, the Ittihad-e-Islami.

Wahhabism In Russia The breakdown and eventual collapse of the Soviet Union opened up another front for Saudi Wahhabism. In 1990, after Islam had been suppressed for years by the Soviet regime, mosques were springing up across Central Asia: fifty new mosques were erected in Kyrgyzstan, whereas just fifteen had gone up the year before; thirty mosques went up in Turkmenistan, after only five the previous year. The pattern repeated itself in other Muslim republics.

Wahhabism In America Since the mid-1960s, Saudi-led Wahhabi organizations have been active in the U.S. The Muslim Students Association (MSA), founded in 1961 at the University of Illinois, frequently features publications of the World Assembly of Muslim Youth (WAMY) on its website. The main works of Wahhabism, including an English translation of Muhammad ibn Abdul Wahhab's *Book of Tawhid*, have also been featured on the website of the University of Southern California MSA chapter.

A Sufi Muslim critic of the "Wahhabization of the Islamic movement" in America, has traced the social and intellectual story of the MSA and other US Muslim movements in the 1960s. The MSA was initiated by Muslims from the Indian subcontinent who were followers of Mawdudi and Arab students who identified with the Muslim Brotherhood and the ideas of Sayyid Qutb. And as one observer remarked, during the 1960s and 1970s "no criticism of Saudi Arabia would be tolerated at the annual conventions of MSA," for during this period, "official approval of Wahhabism remained strong.'"

Back in the Middle East in the 1970s, Mawdudi and the Muslim Brotherhood enjoyed increasing Saudi financial backing. Many Egyptian Muslim Brothers who fled Nasser in the 1960s made fortunes in Saudi Arabia and Qatar before moving to southern California. But while they were refugees in the Gulf, they became Wahhabis.

In the late 1970s, as Muslims returned to their religion, they became active in the Islamic Society of North America (ISNA), which was established in 1981. At the same time, ISNA Muslims rejected Sufism, which could have been the result of Wahhabi influence. These ISNA leadership had been active in MSA or had links with the Muslim World League.

To spread Wahhabism in the US, the Saudis used a tool that had proven very effective in other parts of the world: MONEY. The North American Islamic Trust (NAIT) safeguarded the assets of both the MSA and INSA.

NAIT also helped Muslim communities build mosques, and in the area NAIT became highly dependent on Saudi funding.

A knowledgeable source familiar with Saudi connections in America estimated that half the mosques and Islamic schools in the US were built with Saudi money.

The main question that arises from these contributions is whether those who accept Saudi funds feel pressured to adhere to Wahhabism. The Saudi embassy in Washington has denied that such strings are attached in Saudi donations.

NAIT has a definite religious perspective. Its book service shows something of its orientation; it promotes the writing of the founder of Wahhabism and the works of Sayyid Qutb and Mawlana Mawdudi.

During the war against the Soviet occupation of Afghanistan, the US became an important center for fund-raising campaigns on behalf of the Saudi-backed Afghan Arabs. Between 1985 and 1989, Abdullah Azzam, working out of Pakistan, actually set up support networks in the US. He visited dozens of American cities, spreading his philosophy of jihad. He set up major fund-raising offices, called Alkifah Centers, in Atlanta, Boston, Chicago, Brooklyn, Jersey City, Pittsburgh, and Tucson; thirty other American cities had subsidiary offices.

One of Azzam's most important protégés in the US was a Saudi national, who, as a student at the University of Arizona, was president of the University's Muslim Student Association, and in 1983-1984, he served as the president of the Islamic Center in Tucson. Soon he was drawn to join the Afghan struggle; in 1985 he left the US. In the mid- 1980s, he served the Afghan mujahideen as one of the heads of the Saudi Red Crescent Society in Pakistan, where he worked directly with Abdulla Azzam and Osama bin Laden.

In the early 1990s, the Islamic Center in Tucson moved to Islamic extremism; rhetoric creeping into Friday sermons, delivered during prayers, urged its members to defend Islam from the "infidels." There were signs that it had become an al-Qaeda recruiting center.

Wadih el-Hage, a naturalized US citizen who came from a Lebanese Christian background, and converted to Islam, joined the Tucson mosque, and would later become Osama bin Laden's personal secretary in Sudan and be convicted of plotting the simultaneous 1998 bombings of the US embassies in Kenya and Tanzania.

Hans Hanjour, a Saudi student from Taif, attended the University of Arizona, joined the Islamic Center of Tucson in 1991, returned to

Saudi Arabia for 15 months, returned to the US to attend flight school in Scottsdale, AZ. Five years later, he piloted American Airlines Flight 77 on September 11, 2001, into the Pentagon, killing 184 Americans.

The Institute of Islamic and Arabic Science Fairfax, VA, a branch of Imam Muhammad bin Saud Islamic University that trains more than four hundred students to serve as religious leaders in US mosques, has released such Saudi texts as the *True Religion*. It was printed by the Saudi Arabian Ministry of Islamic Affairs and Endowments, which claims that "Judaism and Christianity are deviant religions" and states that befriending "the Unbelievers" negates Islam. Another text published in the US, *A Muslim's Relations with Non-Muslims, Enmity or Friendship?*, describes those who call for brotherhood and equality among religions as "parasites" and states that the Quran "forbade taking Jews and Christians as friends."

Global Patterns Of Wahhabism

When one looks at how Saudi Islamic activism functioned in different parts of the world, several patterns repeat themselves.

First, the main instruments for this activism were Saudi Arabia's huge Islamic charity organizations – the Muslim World League; its operating arm, the International Islamic Relief Organization (IIRO); al-Haramain; and the World Assembly of Muslim Youth (WAMY). Since their inception, these organizations have been headed by individuals who came from the apex of the Saudi Arabian power structure – including government ministers and members of the Saudi *ulama*.

Second, the geopolitical interests of the Saudi state were not the only factors driving Saudi Islamic activism. In Afghanistan, the Saudis backed the groups who were ideologically closest to Wahhabism. The *ulama* in Saudi Arabia were key in convincing the Saudi leadership to support the Taliban.

Third, across the globe, the Saudi charities promoted terrorism. The IIRO and WAMY assisted the extreme Palestinian group Hamas. Osama bin Laden's brother-in-law Muhammad Jamal Khalifa headed the IIRO's office in the Philippines, through which he assisted the Abu Sayyaf terrorist organization. Muhammad al-Zawahiri, brother of al-Qaeda's Ayman al Zawahiti, worked for IIRO in Tirana, Albania – but, behind the scenes, he was working for an extremist Egyptian organization tied to al-Qaeda.

The based Benevolence International was tied to militant groups in Algeria and Egypt; its offices in Sarajevo were suspected of backing terrorist activities. And, as noted, when a NATO force raided the Sarajevo offices of the Saudi High Commission for Aid to Bosnia in 2001, they found photographs of potential terrorist targets in Washington, DC.

There are two ways of interpreting Saudi charities' global involvement in terrorism: first, that these organizations were victims of determined terrorist groups who penetrated the charities and used them as a front; or, alternatively, that the charities were rogue operations.

If the charities were linked to terrorist groups in only one or even two locations, then the first argument might be plausible. But, because the Saudi charities have been linked to terrorist groups all around the world, it is more than likely that these Saudi-headquartered organizations made a conscious decision to back international terrorism.

For Saudi Arabia, this worldwide financial network was not about terrorism, but rather about jihad. And what began in Afghanistan supporting Muslims rebelling against their Soviet oppressors – evolved in the 1990s into a much wider global struggle involving the Balkans, Tajikistan, Uzbekistan, Kashmir and parts of Russia. The multi-national terrorist organization, al Qaeda, emerged out of these conflicts, and because the Saudis had supplied not just money in many of these struggles but also manpower, it was no surprise that Saudi nationals would eventually represent the largest component of the al-Qaeda network.

America would become the target of the new Jihad. The addition of the US to the list of potential adversaries was a direct by-product of the 1991 Gulf War.

SUMMARY

The truth about Saudi Arabia's relationship with Islam, the introduction of Wahhabism to Islam by its founder, Muhammad ibn Abdul Wahhab, in the mid-eighteenth century, the acceptance, rejection, then acceptance as the true motivation of Islam by Saudi Arabia, as we know it, is discussed in this Chapter.

Muhammad ibn Abdul Wahhab found that the Islamic faith had strayed away from its true intended mission of spreading the message of Allah as stated in the Quran. In Chapter 3, I pointed out the flaws in their faith that I felt had to be changed because it was radical. Wahhabism adds a new dimension to radicalism and forces Muslims to abide or be eliminated.

Osama bin Laden, like the 15 Saudis who participated in the criminal operations of September 11, seems to have been the pure product of his Wahhabi schooling. While Saudi Arabia is officially a state allied with America, it also has been one of the main supporters of Islamic fundamentalism because of its financing of schools following the intransigent Wahhabi doctrine. Saudi-backed madrasas in Pakistan and Afghanistan have played a significant role in the strengthening of radical Islam in the Mideast.

The sub-titles of this chapter tells the story of events that lead us into the next chapter of Jihad, Shariah Law and the Caliphate.

9-11	Oil Weapon
Wahhabism	Radicalism - Ideology
Ikhwan	Money-Oil , Saudi Power
A New Era	Muslim World League
The Oil Weapon	Muslim Brotherhood
Militant Jihad	Azzam's Ideology of Jihad
Wahhabism's Global Reach	Wahhabism In Russia
Wahhabism in America	Wahhabism In America
Hatred and Terror	Global Patterns of Wahhabism

My charge against Islam as being a radical group of terrorists is made stronger in this chapter and the next. Hopefully, the Administration will wake up and see why appeasing the enemy is not in our best interest.

The next Summary is on Page 104.

Chapter 7
Jihad - Shariah Law - Caliphate

Jihad

Jihad is the verbal noun of the Arabic verb, *jahada*, meaning "to endeavor, to strike, to struggle." It is used to denote an effort toward a commendable aim. In religious contexts, it can mean the struggle against one's evil inclinations or efforts toward the moral uplift of society or toward the spread of Islam.

This last undertaking can be peaceful ("jihad of the tongue" or "*jihad* of the pen"), in accordance with Sura 16:125 of the Quran ("Call thou to the way of the Lord with wisdom and admonition, and dispute with them in the better way"), or involve the use of force ("*jihad* of the sword") as mentioned in Sura 2:193 ("Fight them until there is no persecution and the religion is God's then if they give over, there shall be no enmity save for evildoers").

In pious and mystical circles, spiritual and moral jihad is emphasized. This they call "greater *jihad*" on the strength of the following tradition (*hadith*) of the prophet Muhammad: "Once, having returned from one of his campaigns, the Prophet said: 'We have now returned from the lesser *jihad* (i.e., fighting) to the greater *jihad.*'"

In view of the wide semantic spectrum of the word *jihad*, it is not correct to equate it with the notion of "holy war." And, where the word *jihad* does refer to armed struggle, that Islam does not distinguish between holy and secular wars. All wars between Muslims and unbelievers and even wars between different Muslim groups would be labeled *jihad*, even if fought for perfectly secular reasons. The religious aspect, then, is reduced to the certainty of the individual warriors that if they are killed they will enter paradise.

Jihad in the Quran and in the Hadith. In cases where the verb *jahada* or its derivatives occur in the Quran, it denotes warfare. Its distribution – and the verb *qatala* ("combat – fight") – reflects the history of the Islamic community. They are often linked with the phrase "in the way of God" (*fi sabil Allah*) to underscore the religious character of the struggle.

Many later verses on jihad order the believers to take part in warfare, promise heavenly reward to those who do, and threaten those who do not with severe punishment in the hereafter. Some verses deal with practical matters such as exemption from military service (9:91, 48:17), fighting during the holy months (2:217) and in the holy territory of Mecca (2:191), the fate of prisoners of war (47:4), safe conduct (9:6), and truce (8:61).

In that the Quranic verses on the relationship between Muslims and non-Muslims give evidence of a clear evolution from peacefulness to enmity and warfare, Muslim scholars argued that this evolution culminated in an unconditional command to fight the unbelievers, as embodied in verses such as 5:9 ("Then when the sacred months are drawn away, slay the idolaters wherever you find them, and take them and confine them, and lie in wait for them at every place of ambush"). The "sword verses" are considered to have repealed all other verse.

There is *hadith* on *jihad*. The *hadiths* deal with the same topics as the Quran but place more emphasis on the excellence of *jihad* as a pious act, on the rewards of martyrdom, and on practical and ethical matters of warfare. A typical *hadith* is: When the Prophet sent out a raiding party, he would say, "Raid in the name of God and in the way of God. Fight those who do not believe in God. Raid! Do not embezzle spoils, do not act treacherously, do not mutilate, and do not kill children."

Jihad in Islamic Law. The central part of this doctrine is that the Muslim community as a whole has the duty to expand the territory and rule of Islam. Consequently, *jihad* is a collective duty of all Muslims, which means that if a sufficient number take part in it, the community has fulfilled its obligation. If the number of participants is inadequate, the sin rests on all Muslims.

After the period of conquests the jurists stipulated that the Muslim ruler, in order to keep the idea of *jihad* alive, ought to organize an expedition into enemy territory once a year. If the enemy attacks Muslim territory, *jihad* becomes an individual duty for all able –bodied inhabitants of the region under attack. Those killed in *jihad* are called *tyrs (shuyhada –shahid)*. Their sins are forgiven and they go straight to paradise.

The aim of *jihad* is "the subjection of the unbelievers" and "the extirpation of unbelief." This is understood in a political way as the extension of Islamic rule over the remaining parts of the world. The peoples thus conquered are not forced to embrace Islam: with payment of a special poll tax (*jizyah*) they can acquire the status of protected minorities and become non-Muslim subjects of the Islamic state (*dhimmis*).

Before the final aim – Muslim domination of the whole world – has been achieved, the situation of war prevails between the Islamic state and the surrounding regions.

The *jihad* chapters in the legal handbooks contain many rules.

Warfare must start with the summons in which the enemies are asked to embrace Islam or accept the status of non-Muslim subjects. Only if they refuse may they be attacked. Other prescriptions concern, as an example, the protection of the lives of non-combatants, the treatment of prisoners of war, and the division of spoils.

Jihad in History. The doctrine of *jihad* has been invoked to justify wars between Muslim and non-Muslim states and even to legitimate wars between Muslims themselves. Adversaries would be branded as heretics or rebels to warrant the application of the *jihad* doctrine. In the 18th and 19th centuries, they were often referred to as *jihad* movements.

Despite their geographical range – from West Africa to Southeast Asia – and the different social, economic, and political causes from which they sprang, they employed the same notions from the Islamic repertoire. *Jihad*, for them meant the struggle within an only nominally Islamic society for the purification of religion and the establishment of a genuine Islamic community.

In concert with the *jihad* doctrine and the obligation of *hijrah*, the duty of Muslims to emigrate from areas controlled by non-Muslims, was frequently appealed to. The notion of a *Mahdi* played a role, either because the leader proclaimed himself as such, or because he was regarded as a minister appointed to prepare the *Mahdi's* advent.

Examples of *jihad* movements are the Wahhabiyah in Arabia, founded by Muhammad ibn Abdul-Wahhab (1703-1787), the Fulbe *jihad* in northern Nigeria led by Usuman dan Fodio (1754-1817), the West African *jihad* movement of Umar Tal (1794-1864) and the *Mahdist* movement of Muhammad Ahmad in the Sudan (1881-1898).

The Contemporary Significance of the Jihad Doctrine. Since the 19th century attempts were made to reinterpret the doctrine of *jihad*. One of the first thinkers to do so was the Indian reformer Sayyid Ahmad

Khan (1817-1898). Believing that the interests of the Indian Muslims would be served best by close cooperation with the British colonizers, he sought to improve relations between both groups. After the 1857 revolt (the so-called Mutiny), the British, who blamed the Muslims even with massive Hindu participation, had favored the latter on the grounds that collaboration with Muslims would pose a security risk because of their allegiance to the doctrine of *jihad*. By offering a new interpretation of the jihad duty, Sayyid Khan wanted to refute these views and prove that Muslims could be loyal subjects of the British Crown. He rejected the theory that the "sword verses" repealed all other verses concerning the relations with non-Muslims. On the basis of the new reading of the Quran, he asserted that *jihad* was obligatory only in the case of "positive oppression or obstruction in the exercise of their faith, impairing the foundation of some of the pillars of Islam." Since the British did not interfere with the Islamic cult, *jihad* against them was not allowed.

In India this interpretation of the jihad doctrine found some support. In the Middle East, however, they did not go so far. Their opinions differed considerably from the classical doctrine. They contended that peaceful coexistence is the normal relationship between Islamic and non-Islamic territory and that *jihad* must be understood as defensive warfare, regardless of whether the aggression on the part of the non-Muslims is directed against religion or not. In their view, *jihad* could be proclaimed against western colonial rule in the Islamic world.

Apart from the conservative trend that contents itself with repeating the classical legal texts, there is the fundamentalist or revivalist tendency, whose adherents want to change the world according to Islamic principles.

The Sixth Pillar

Muslims believe firmly of the five Pillars of Islam: *Shahada* "(I profess that) there is no other god but God and Muhammad is the last messenger of God; *Salat* - five daily prayers: Fajr, Dhuhr, Asr, Maghrib, and Isha'a; *Sawm* - fasting as compensation for repentance (traditionally broken during the month of Ramadan); *Zakat* - practice of charitable giving by Muslims based on accumulated wealth, and is obligatory for all who are able to do so; and *Hajj* - obliged to make the pilgrimage to Mecca at least once in their lifetime if he or she can afford it.

Muslims believe that *Jihad* is the sixth Pillar.

Shariah Law

An Arabic word meaning path - In Islam God's revealed law for human beings. Islam holds that God, as creator, desires human beings to live in certain ways, and that he has revealed those ways to humans. That revealed laws is known as Shariah. It is distinct from *fiqh*, human attempts to formulate God's law.

God has revealed Shariah through two sources, the *Quran*, God's revelations to the Prophet Muhammad, and the *Hadith*, reports about what the Prophet said and did that have been carefully scrutinized to ensure their accuracy. According to these sources there are some actions that God requires human beings to perform and some that God absolutely forbids. Other actions fall somewhere in between, as being either preferable to do, preferable to avoid, or neutral. Although the Quran and Hadith contain Shariah, human beings must interpret them.

In Shi'ite Islam the proper interpretation is associated especially with the descendants of the Prophet, the Shi'ite Imams, and in practice today with religious authorities known as Ayatollahs.

Shi'ite's believe that Muhammad had indeed chosen a successor: his first cousin, son-in-law, and early convert, 'Ali ibn Abi Talib. They move on in life feeling that they are the chosen ones.

Shi'ite vs. Sunni: *Shiites represent about 16% of Muslims normally found in Iran, Iraq and Bahrain, while Sunnis are 84%, or the rest of the Muslims who are not Shiite located in the Arabian states. Shiites believe that they are the direct descendants of Muhammad through Ali, the son-in-law of Muhammad.*

In Sunni Islam interpretation is the job of legal scholars or jurists. These jurists try to determine precisely what the texts mean. They also reason from analogy to part because situations arise today that could not have been anticipated in Arabia at the time of God's final revelation. An individual jurist may issue a *fatwa*, a statement of what the law requires. Such a legal opinion is instructive, but it is not binding. More binding is the unanimous consensus of jurists. A verse in the Quran says that the community of the faithful will never agree on error.

Ideally, Shariah constitutes the law of a Muslim state. In practice, most Muslim states have used Shariah in some areas, such as personal law, and made their own laws in other areas, such as criminal law. In recent decades Muslim feminists have argued that traditional rules that disadvantaged women are not Shariah but improper interpretations on the part of past legal scholars. Fundamentalist Muslims take a different position. They condemn the secularism that they see around them as an abandonment of God's revelation and advocate the application of Shariah in most or all spheres of life.

Caliphate

The office of "successor" to the Prophet Muhammad as the leader of the Muslim community is a uniquely Islamic institution. The Anglicization *Caliphate* is preferable to inadequate translations of the term *Khilafah*.

Upon Muhammad's death in 632 CE there was in existence a self-governing, powerful Islamic community, or *ummah*. It had been shaped by the Prophet in conformity with the revelations he had received, and by the end of his life, his temporal as well as his spiritual authority was unassailable: he was the governor of the *ummah*, an arbitrator of disputes within it, the commander of its military forces, and its principal strategist. He had deputized others as his representatives to distant tribes and regions. The term *Khaltfah* in the pre-Islamic sense of "deputy" was apparently used in reference to these assignees.

To the *ummah*, the Prophet's death was a shocking, even inconceivable event. The Muslims were suddenly bereft of divine guidance, the source of Muhammad's charismatic authority. Yet they were sufficiently imbued with the Islamic vision to persevere in efforts to shape the ideal society embodied in that moral imperative.

But who was to lead this society? What was to be his authority? The caliphate, the expression of the temporal leadership of all Muslims conceived as a single community, was the institutional answer. It had emerged *ad hoc,* in response to a crisis. Evolving practice framed theoretical constructions, especially in the absence of any agreed Quranic foundation. Thus the conduct of those holding the office, the caliphs, elicited sharp and continuing controversy over not only individual moral qualities but also the character of the institution itself.

The forces at work in this controversy may be divided for the purposes of analysis into Islamic theories of the caliphate and historical influences on the institution.

Classical Theories of the Caliphate. The overall Sunni view of the origins of the caliphate is that Muhammad left no instructions for the future leadership of the *ummah*. The community desperately required an acknowledged leader. The innermost core of the Muslims responded by acclaiming as their leader one of the earliest of their number and certainly among the most prestigious, Abu Bakr (632-634). Whether he was actually proclaimed *khaltfat rasul Allah* ("caliph of the messenger of God") is unclear, but all Sunnis regard him as the first caliph.

His role was to lead the *ummah* in peace and in war as the Prophet had done, and to lead the ritual prayers and conduct the pilgrimage, both of which duties he had previously performed on Muhammad's behalf. Absent from this formulation was the prophetic role that had clothed Muhammad's acts with impeccable authority. Theoretically, a divinely guided community of Muslims selected the early Sunni caliphs, while its act of acclamation, the *bay'ah,* constituted an elective ideal not in concurrence with subsequent dynasticism.

The Sunni theory required that a caliph be an adult male from the Quraysh, the leading tribe of Mecca. Soundness of mind and body, knowledge of religion, piety, and probity are frequently listed among Sunni criteria. Caliphal prerogatives were to lead the prayer, to be recognized in the Friday sermon as the leader of all Muslims, to coin money, to command the army, and to receive on behalf of the *ummah* a fifth of all booty. Later, the Abbasid caliphs (750-1258) claimed for themselves the right to wear the presumed mantle of the Prophet, a sacred relic in their possession.

Sunnis generally describe the caliph's duties as follows: to defend the domain of Islam and to extend it if possible, to uphold the shariah, the prescribed conduct for a Muslim, to ensure law and order so that Muslims might observe the shariah in peace and security, to collect canonical taxes, and generally to administer the *ummah* in consultation with selected counselors.

The Shiite conception of the caliphate differs from the Sunni in the manner of origination and the consequences flowing therefrom. Out of certain verses of the Quran and from selected hadith (reports of the Prophet's words of deeds), the Shiah adduce that Muhammad had indeed chosen a successor: his first cousin, son-in-law, and early convert, 'Ali ibn Abi Talib. According to the Shiah, a conspiracy among the companions of the Prophet denied 'Ali his rightful position, plunging the community into error the instant Muhammad died. That the prophet had himself selected 'Ali establishes to Shi'ah satisfaction a leadership of far greater charismatic authority than the Sunni version, a leadership that for most of the Shiite grew to incorporate impeccability and infallible interpretation of scripture.

'Ali did become the fourth caliph, the last of the so-called Rashidun or "rightly guided" caliphs, but his designation by the assassins of his predecessor, 'Uthman ibn 'Affan (644-656) of the clan of Umayyah, precipitated a civil war that taxed forever the fabric of the community.

When 'Ali was killed in 661, the caliphate was passed to the Umayyads from 661 to750. The Shiah would thereafter cleave to the view that only the 'Alids, 'Ali's progeny, could claim the caliphate; their claim alone was divinely sanctioned. The inability of the Shiahs ever to agree on a particular candidate among Ali's descendants condemned their movement to martyrdom, factionalism, and futility.

The conflict between 'Ali and the Umayyads spawned a third interpretation of the caliphate, that of the *Kharijis*. In the view of these numerically few but very active dissidents, hostile to both parties following the civil war, the caliph was liable for deposition should he deviate an iota from Muhammad's practice. The Kharijis thus depreciated the office to no better than a tribal chieftainship. Arab nomadic groups were, in fact, the milieu from which they drew their support.

By the late 19th century the force of European imperialism had sparked a revival of the caliphate in a new form that engendered as much controversy among Muslims as had the classical version. The Ottoman sultan, ruling a sprawling empire threatened by European powers, sought to elevate his prestige and retain a link to his lost Muslim subjects by recasting the caliphate into a spiritual office. This device appealed to Muslims under colonial rule, such as in India, Tsarist Russia, the Malay Peninsula, and the Indonesian archipelago. Even in British-occupied Egypt it elicited a favorable response. But within the Ottoman empire, non-Muslim nationalists struggling for independence regarded the revived concept of the caliphate as an instrument to marshal Muslim support for their suppression.

By the eve of the First World War this view was shred even by some Muslim Arabs who decried the Ottoman caliphate as a sham lacking the slightest trace of a Quraysh pedigree. Both Islamic reformers and Muslim nationalists reviled the Ottoman sultan/caliph and, citing classical scholars to support their contention, characterized the Rashidun as the only true caliphs.

In retrospect, it is not surprising that the most secular of the nationalist movements in Muslim countries, the Turkish, should have abolished the Ottoman caliphate in 1924; at the time it came as a shock to the entire Muslim world. The Indian Khilafat Conference (1919-1933), advocating self-rule for Indian Muslims because they owed spiritual allegiance to the caliph, found its cause hopelessly undercut. Muslims demanding independence from colonialism had to revise their strategy once they overcame their disappointment.

In the newly independent Arab world a contest for the caliphate emerged, but the effort to revive the "true" caliphate was short-lived. Three conferences over a brief span (1926-1931) broke up in disarray. It was soon apparent that new nation-states opposed the restoration of such a vaguely defined but potentially influential institution unless their own governments could control it.

The quickened religious pulse in the Islamic world today has evoked no noticeable inclination to revive the concept of the caliphate. It would seem that however much Muslims may desire a greater sense of unity, any expression of such sentiment is unlikely to assume the caliphal form.

Mahdi

The second Coming of Christ for Christians has a comparable that can be found in Islam, probably owing to Christian influence. While the Quran has Allah as the judge on the Day of Judgment, later Muslim tradition introduces certain preparatory events before that day.

Muhammad is reported to have said that the last day of the world will be prolonged in order that a ruler of his family may defeat all enemies of Islam. This ruler is called the Mahdi, "the rightly guided one." Other traditions say that he will fill the world with justice as it is now filled with wrong, an apparent echo of ancient kingship ideology.

Some identify the Mahdi with Jesus, who is supposed to appear before the end of the world to defeat al-Dajjal ("the deceiver"), the false messiah, or antichrist. Such traditions were utilized by founders of new dynasties and other political or religious leaders, especially among the Shiites. The last example was the rebel leader Muhammad Ahmad of Sudan, who from 1883 temporarily held back the British influence in this area.

We Should Be Concerned

From the above narration of Jihad, Caliph, Shariah Law, the Caliphate and the Mahdi, we come to the present day threats introduced in the article that follows by Michael Evans in 2007.

With our current Administration in Washington, we are hard-pressed for leadership since we do not know of the President's religious leanings. We have videos of him declaring he is a Muslim, but woe be us as to why he doesn't make a public announcement of it.

SUMMARY

In this chapter, We discussed

Jihad - The Sixth Pillar
Shariah Law
Caliphate
Mahdi

You can Google "The Second Coming of the Mahdi"

After reading the article, (and the chapter when you have time), it becomes clear that this chapter accents the radicalism of Islam to the point of near insanity.

Couple that with the revelations in the previous chapters about Islam, the Comparative Religions, Minorities and Racial Differences, the Saudi Arabians and Wahhabism, and you can conclude that we are rounding out a "fear factor" of a "Clear and Present Danger" that America is facing.

If I were President, my eyes would be fixed on the threat that the article, "The Second Coming of the Mahdi," suggests.

Mahmoud Ahmadinejad believes that the world will come to its end with the Coming of the Mahdi, and that the end would be triggered by a huge burst of flames and fire, as in a nuclear explosion *(Armageddon)*.

Based on his radical way of thinking, that the "huge burst of flames" marks the end, he is trying to end the world so that the Muslims will ascend to Paradise and the rest of the world, us - the non-believers, will be scourged in hell.

This book will let the Leaders of the Arab countries know that we are aware of the premise of the article, and that "If I Were President," Congress, my Cabinet, Administration and the Joint Chiefs of Staff will know, in advance, when to eliminate the threat.

And, we will thank the European countries for the "heads up" warning.

The next Summary is on page 115.

Chapter 8

Can A Good Muslim
Be A Good American?

This chapter takes into account all of the peculiarities of Islam that formulates a plan to stop the Islamic Movement in America.

Let's review what we've assembled.

Christians In The World

Two Billion One Hundred Million Christians scattered in most countries of the world. That's a little more than 30% of the world's population. One out of three people in the world is a Christian.

In America, there are 260 Million Christians representing almost 87% of the population. Unfortunately, the numbers are dwindling. We are losing many Black Christians who are being converted to Islam.

There are around 21 denominations of Christians in America. It would seem like if there were a way to reduce that number so that Christians can focus on the message of Jesus, it would make it less problematic for Blacks to leave Christianity.

Muslims In The World

One Billion Two Hundred Million Muslims worldwide. That's 20% of the world population – one out of every five people in the world is a Muslim.

There are 10 Million Muslims in America. That's 3% of our population. At their current rate of growth, in eight years, they should represent over 50% of our population. That would be a problem. They would insist that America be converted to Shariah Law. They would have the votes to make it happen. America would be at their mercy.

The Breakdown

The chart below lists the 125 Countries alphabetically, the percentage of its population that is Muslim and the total number of Muslims by the Millions.

The countries that have 3% or fewer Muslims are: Argentina, Brazil, Cambodia, Canada, Croatia, Gabon, Greece, Hong Kong, Italy, Japan, Netherlands, Norway, Rwanda, Slovenia, South Africa, Sweden, United Kingdom and the United States.

Country	%	# x M	Country	%	# x M	Country	%	# x M
Afghanistan	100	28.072	Djibouti	94	.428	Liberia	30	2.110
Albania	75	3.249	Egypt	94	63.576	Libya	100	5.446
Algeria	99	29.184	Equa Guinea	25	.432	Lesotho	10	1.972
Angola	25	10.343	Entrea	80	3.428	Macedonia	30	2.105
Argentina	2	34.674	Ethiopia	65	57.172	Madagascar	20	13.671
Aruba	5	.068	Fiji	11	.783	Malawi	35	9.453
Australia	2	18.261	France	7	58.318	Malaysia	52	19.963
Azerbaijan	93	7.670	Gabon	1	1.173	Maldives	100	.271
Bahrain	100	.590	Gambia	90	1.205	Mali	90	9.654
Benin	15	5.710	Gaza Strip	98	.924	Malta	14	.376
Bangladesh	85	123.085	Georgia	11	5.220	Mauritania	100	2.337
Bhutan	5	1.825	Germany	3.4	83.537	Mauritius	19	1.141
Bosnia	40	2.660	Ghana	30	17.700	Mayotte	99	.101
Botswana	5	1.480	Gibraltar	8	.029	Mongolia	4	2.497
Brazil	0.6	162.670	Greece	1.5	10.540	Morocco	98	29.780
Brunei	63	.300	Guinea	95	7.413	Mozambique	29	17.878
Bulgaria	14	8.614	Guinea-Bissa	70	1.152	Namibia	5	1.678
Burkina Fas	50	10.626	Guyana	15	.713	Nepal	4	22.095
Burma	10	45.978	Hong Kong	1	6.306	Netherlands	3	15.569
Burundi	20	5.946	India	14	952.108	Niger	91	9.114
Cambodia	1	10.866	Indonesia	95	206.612	Nigeria	75	103.913
Cameroon	55	14.263	Iran	99	66.095	Norway	1.5	4.439
Canada	1.5	28.821	Iraq	97	21.423	Oman	100	2.187
Cntrl Africa	55	3.277	Israel	14	5.423	Pakistan	97	129.276
Chad	85	6.979	Italy	1	57.461	Panama	4	2.656
China	11	1,210.008	Japan	1	125.450	Philippines	14	74.481
Comoros	86	.570	Jordan	95	4.213	Qatar	100	.548
Congo	15	2.528	Kazakstan	51	16.917	Reunion	20	.680
Cote d'Ivoir	60	14.763	Kenya	30	28.178	Romania	20	21.658
Croatia	1.2	5.005	Kuwait	89	1.951	Russia	18	148.179
Cyprus	33	.745	Kyrgyzstan	76	4.530	Rwanda	1	6.854
Denmark	2		Lebanon	70	3.777	Saudi Arabia	100	19.410

Country	%	# x M	Country	%	# x M	Country	%	# x M
Senegal	95	9.093	Swaziland	10	.999	Uganda	36	20.159
SerbiaMont	19	10.615	Sweden	3.6	9.800	United Arab	96	3.058
SierraLeone	65	4.794	Syria	90	15.609	UK England	2.7	58.490
Singapore	17	3.397	Tajikistan	85	5.917	U.S.America	3	267.477
Slovenia	1	1.952	Tanzania	65	29.059	Uzbekistan	88	23.419
Somalia	100	9.640	Thailand	14	58.852	West Bank	75	1.428
SouthAfrica	2	41.744	Togo	55	4.571	WestSahara	100	.223
Spain	4		Trinidad	12	1.273	Yemen	99	13.484
Sri Lanka	9	18.554	Tunisia	98	9.020	Zaire	10	46.499
Sudan	85	31.548	Turkey	99	62.485	Zambia	15	9.160
Suriname	25	.437	Turkmenistan	87	4.150	Zimbabwe	15	11.272

Since it can be proven that the Quran and the Islamic doctrines are flawed, which makes Islam a questionable religion, if it is even a religion, we should pursue the course of removal of Islam from America.

We are in the 10 percentile bracket, at present. That is to say that we are a part of the ten percent of the nations with the fewest Muslims. While we are at this level, now is the time to take action to force Islam out of our borders.

After we make America Islam-Free, we can help the 17 countries listed above, if they wish, then all the other countries, if they so desire.

A Quick Lesson on Islam

Slavery, Terrorism and Islam: Historical Roots and Contemporary Threat
Islam is not a religion, nor is it a cult. In its true form, it is a total, 100% system of life. Islam has religious, legal, political, economic, social, and military components. The religious component is a beard for all of the other components.

Islamization begins when there are sufficient Muslims in a country to agitate for their religious privileges.

When politically correct, tolerant, and culturally diverse societies agree to Muslim demands for their religious privileges, some of the other components tend to creep in as well.

Here's how it works: As long as the Muslim population remains around or under 2% in any given country, they will be for the most part regarded as a peace-loving minority, and not as a threat to other citizens. This is the case in:

Gabon	1%	Italy	1%	Cambodia	1%
Rwanda	1%	Japan	1%	Slovenia	1%
Croatia	1.2%	Norway	1.5%	Canada	1.5%

At 2% to 5%, they begin to proselytize from other ethnic minorities and disaffected groups, often with major recruiting from the jails and among street gangs. This is happening in:

Argentina	2%	Australia	2%	Denmark	2%
So. Africa	2%	United King.	2.7%	United States	3%
Germany	3.4%	Spain	4%	Mongolia	4%

From 5% on, they exercise an inordinate influence in proportion to their percentage of the population. For example, they will push for the introduction of Halal (clean by Islamic standards) food, thereby securing food preparation jobs for Muslims. They will increase pressure on supermarket chains to feature Halal on their shelves -- along with threats for failure to comply. This is occurring in:

Aruba	5%	Bhutan	5%	Botswana	5%
Namibia	5%	France	7%	Gibraltar	8%
Sri Lanka	9%				

At this point, they will work to get the ruling government to allow them to rule themselves (within their ghettos) under Sharia, the Islamic Law. The ultimate goal of Islamists is to establish Sharia law over the entire world.

When Muslims approach 10% of the population, they tend to increase lawlessness as a means of complaint about their conditions. In Paris, we are already seeing car-burnings.

Any non-Muslim action offends Islam and results in uprisings and threats, such as in Amsterdam, with opposition to Muhammad cartoons and films about Islam. Such tensions are seen daily, particularly in Muslim sections in:

Bulgaria	14%	Israel	14%	India	14%
Philipines	14%	Benin	15%	Congo	15%
Comoros	15%	Singapore	17%	Russia	18%

After reaching 20%, nations can expect hair-trigger rioting, jihad militia formations, sporadic killings, and the burnings of Christian churches and Jewish synagogues, such as in:

Burundi	20%	Equa Guinea	25%	Angola	25%
Ghana	30%	Kenya	30%	Cyprus	33%

At 40%, nations experience widespread massacres, chronic terror attacks, and ongoing militia warfare, such as in:

Bosnia	40%	Kazakstan	51%	Malaysia	52%

From 60%, nations experience unfettered persecution of non-believers of all other religions (including non-conforming Muslims), sporadic ethnic cleansing (genocide), use of Sharia Law as a weapon, and Jizyah, the tax placed on infidels, such as in:

Cote d'Ivor	60%	Ethiopia	65%	Lebanon	70%
Guinea	70%	Albania	75%	Kyrgyztan	76%

After 80%, expect daily intimidation and violent jihad, some State-run ethnic cleansing, and even some genocide, as these nations drive out the infidels, and move toward 100% Muslim, such as has been experienced and in some ways is on-going in:

Chad	85%	Indonesia	95%	Egypt	94%
Syria	90%	Tajikistan	85%	Jordan	92%
United Arab	96%	Iraq	97%	Pakistan	97%
Iran	99%	Gaza	98%	Morocco	98%

100% will usher in the peace of 'Dar-es-Salaam' -- the Islamic House of Peace. Here there's supposed to be peace, because everybody is a Muslim, the Madrassas are the only schools, and the Quran is the only word, such as in:

Afghanistan	100%	Saudi Arabia	100%	Somalia	100%
Qatar	100%	West Sahara	100%	Libya	100%

Unfortunately, peace is never achieved, as in these 100% Muslim states the most radical Muslims intimidate and spew hatred, and satisfy their blood lust by killing less radical Muslims, for a variety of reasons.

'Before I was nine, I had learned the basic canon of Arab life. It was me against my brother; me and my brother against our father; my family against my cousins and the clan; the clan against the tribe; the tribe against the world, and all of us against the infidel. --
Leon Uris, 'The Haj'

It is important to understand that in some countries, with well under 100% Muslim populations, such as France, the minority Muslim populations live in ghettos, within which they are 100% Muslim, and within which they live by Sharia Law. The national police do not even enter these ghettos. There are no national courts, nor schools, nor non-Muslim religious facilities. In such situations, Muslims do not integrate into the community at large. The children attend Madrassas. They learn only the Quran. To even associate with an infidel is a crime punishable with death. Therefore, in some areas of certain nations, Muslim Imams and extremists exercise more power than the national average would indicate.

Today's 1.2 billion Muslims make up 20% of the world's population. But their birth rates dwarf the birth rates of Christians, Hindus, Buddhists, Jews, and all other believers. Muslims will exceed 50% of the world's population by the end of this century.

Maybe this is why our American Muslims are so quiet and not speaking out about any atrocities. **Can a good Muslim be a good American?** This question was forwarded to a friend who worked in Saudi Arabia for 20 years. The following is his reply:

Theologically	No	Because his allegiance is to Allah, the moon god of Arabia.
Religiously	No	Because no other religion is accepted by his Allah except Islam. (Quran 2:256)
Scripturally	No	Because his allegiance is to the five Pillars of Islam and the Quran.
Geographically	No	Because his allegiance is to Mecca, to which he turns in prayer five times a day.
Socially	No	Because his allegiance to Islam forbids him to make friends with Christians or Jews.
Politically	No	Because he must submit to the mullahs (spiritual leaders), who teach annihilation of Israel and destruction of America, the great Satan.
Domestically	No	Because he is instructed to marry four women and to beat and scourge his wife when she disobeys him (Quran 4:34)
Intellectually	No	Because he cannot accept the American Constitution since it is based on Biblical principles and he believes the Bible to be corrupt.
Philosophically	No	Because Islam, Muhammad, and the Quran do not allow freedom of religion and expression. Democracy and Islam cannot co-exist. Every Muslim government is either dictatorial or autocratic.
Spiritually	No	Because when we declare "one nation under God," the Christian's God is loving and kind, while **Allah is NEVER referred to as Heavenly Father**, nor is he ever called "Love" in the Quran's 99 excellent names.

Therefore, after much study and deliberation - we must be very suspicious of ALL MUSLIMS in this country. They obviously cannot be both 'good'

Muslims **and** good Americans. The religious war is bigger than we know or understand.

Can a Muslim be a good soldier? Army Major Nidal Malik Hasan, opened fire at Ft. Hood and Killed 13. He is a good Muslim!

Footnote: The Muslims said they will destroy us from within. Our job is to make them fail.

FREEDOM IS NOT FREE! WE WILL OVERCOME
THE MUSLIM BROTHERHOOD AND ISLAM!

Allies In The Middle East

Israel: The close relationship that we have enjoyed will be renewed with pride and solidified for all future generations.

We will be sure to check the allegiance of our future Presidents to our allies. May that be sacredly honored from this day forward.

India: With a 14% Muslim population, we will strengthen our ties with our friends in India. We will negotiate and help as it wishes.

Lebanon: It appears that Lebanon will be carrying a heavy load in the shaping of mid-eastern alliances. We look forward to the alliance that will help us forge ahead toward the future.

A Word of Caution

To Iran, Syria, Palestine, Saudi Arabia and Arab countries aligned with them, we urge you to find a way to negotiate peace with our allies, (Israel, India, Lebanon).

When this issue of the legitimacy of Islam in America is resolved, it would behoove all the countries, not yet on the list of Allies of America, to find a Place with a Round Table where we can discuss working relations with each other.

It is our hope that between now and the time that the new Administration takes office, our efforts will be toward furthering peaceful relations with all countries of the world, rather than having private meetings with the select few, which up until now, has not proven to be successful.

EUROPEAN LIFE DIED IN AUSCHWITZ

This article was written by Spanish writer Sebastian Vilar Rodrigez and published in a Spanish newspaper on Jan. 15, 2008. It doesn't take much imagination to extrapolate the message to the rest of Europe - and possibly to the rest of the world.

Mr. Rodrigez discovered a terrible truth - that Europe killed six million Jews and replaced them with twenty million Muslims.

In Auschwitz, they burned a culture, thought, creativity, talent. They destroyed the chosen people who produced great and wonderful people who changed the world.

Under pretense of tolerance, and because they wanted to prove to themselves that they were cured of the disease of racism, they opened their gates to 20 million Muslims, who brought them stupidity and ignorance, religious extremism and lack of tolerance, crime and poverty, due to an unwillingness to work and support their families with pride.

Mr. Rodriqez claims that they exchanged the pursuit of peace of the Jews of Europe and their talent for a better future for their children, their determined clinging to life because life is holy, for those who pursue death, for people consumed by the desire for death for themselves and others, for our children and theirs.

STAY IN TOUCH WITH THE WORLD

A lot of Americans have become so insulated from reality that they imagine America can suffer defeat without any inconvenience to them.

Absolutely No Profiling! What? These events are actual events from history. Remember?

1. 1968, Bobby Kennedy was shot and killed;
2. In 1972 at the Munich Olympics, athletes were kidnapped and massacred;
3. In 1979, the U.S. embassy in Iran was taken over;
4. During the 1980s many Americans were kidnapped in Lebanon;
5. In 1983 the U.S. Marine barracks in Beirut was blown up;
6. In 1985 the cruise ship Achille Lauro was hijacked. A 70-year-old US passenger was murdered and thrown overboard in his wheelchair;
7. In 1985 TWA flight 847 was hijacked at Athens and a U.S. Navy diver trying to rescue passengers was murdered;

8. In 1988, Pan Am Flight 103 was bombed;
9. In 1993 the World Trade Center was bombed the first time;
10. In 1998 U.S. Embassies in Kenya and Tanzania were bombed;
11. On 9/11/01, four airliners were hijacked. Two were used as missiles to take out the World Trade Center. Of the remaining two, one crashed into the U.S. Pentagon and the other was diverted and crashed by the passengers. Thousands of people were killed;
12. In 2002 the United States fought a war in Afghanistan against;
13. In 2002 reporter Daniel Pearl was kidnapped and murdered; All by male Muslims between the ages of 17 and 40.
14. 14. And now we can add: In 2009, 31 people wounded and 13 American Soldiers murdered on base at Fort Hood by a Major who was known as . . . A Muslim male extremist between the age of 17 and 40.

So, to ensure we Americans never offend anyone, particularly fanatics intent on killing us, airport security screeners will no longer be allowed to profile certain people. They must conduct random searches of 80-year-old women, little kids, airline pilots with proper identification, secret agents who are members of the President's security detail, 85-year olds **but leave Muslim males between the ages 17 and 40 alone lest they be guilty of profiling.**

Extremist Cleric: Time For Islamic State In America

An extremist Muslim cleric was planning a March rally at the White House in hopes of sparking a revolution that would turn the United States into an Islamic State.

According to the Daily Mall newspaper, the Cleric told a reporter that "The event is a rally, a call for the Sharia, a call for Muslims to rise up and establish the Islamic State In America."

The Cleric says he expects the rally to draw thousands of supporters. The event will be sponsored by the New York-based extremist group Islamic Thinkers. The Cleric says that "the flag of Islam will fly over the White House" and that Americans "are the biggest criminals in the world today."

SUMMARY

The question was: **Can a good Muslim be a good American?**

In this chapter, I tried to condense the subject matter to provide you with the answers you need to decide for yourself whether I am over reacting to the threat of Islam.

But, try as I may to find a medium ground for the Muslims, I have to agree with Dr. Hammond, that there is no way that a Good Muslim *(if there is such a thing)* could be a Good American.

Theologically
Religiously
Scripturally
Geographically
Socially
Politically
Domestically
Intellectually
Philosophically
Spiritually

Dr Hammond discussed ten different categories, listed at left, of whether a Muslim can coexist to be a good American. And, in each category, the Muslim would fail to meet the standards.

The answer was NO in each case because of the way the Muslim mind has been taught by the Quran and Madrassas.

It would take too long to retrain their thinking for them to be considered Good Americans.

By reading the Quran, it is difficult to understand how anyone would want to be a Muslim. But, it seems that once a Muslim accepts the doctrine and Quran, it is difficult to adjust otherwise.

So, from "understanding Islam," comparing their ideology with that of the other "religions of the world," looking at the "minority issues" in America and elsewhere, considering Saudi Arabia as a major contributing factor to the "origin of terror," coupled with "jihad, shariah law, and the caliphate," and, finally, trying to determine their capability of becoming "good Americans," – it is easy to conclude that the answer is NO, and to consider them a threat that must be removed from our borders.

Now, with extremist Clerics saying that "It's time for an Islamic State in America," and looking at events in history since 1968 that were attacks by Muslims, the threat becomes overwhelming.

In the article "European Life Died In Auschwitz," it is a sad commentary of the holocaust, which most of Islam refuse to accept happened. But, the anger of the author of what has happened to Europe can be felt.

The next Summary is on Page 133

Chapter 9
The Challenge

Reading the dozen recommended books and three Qurans that I did, I have managed to come up with more questions now than when I started out

I am impressed with what the authors said about the formation of the religion of Islam, but I am not impressed with the perception of Islam.

The differences in translations and expressions of the Qurans that I have read lead me to believe that I need to ease my remarks about Islam and the Muslims. I am at the mercy of interpretations by the three authors and how they verbalize themselves in their translations to English.

In each version of the Quran the translation varies slightly. The Sura numbers are not necessarily the same, but the conclusion is synonymous. Therefore, I will charge on with the Challenge.

Having said that, would I be an Unbeliever? If so, would I be subject to punishment according to the threats of the Quran?

Outline

The Challenge is expressed in five categories:

Yahweh vs Allah,

Bible vs. Quran

Jesus vs. Muhammad

America vs Islam, and,

Israel vs Islam.

Where comments are made about the Bible vs Quran, compare the comments to the Suras that were extracted and shown in Chapter 3, Understanding Islam.

Yahweh vs Allah (The God of Israel vs. The God of Islam)

Yahweh would not ask me to kill anyone just because he disagrees with my faith. So why did Allah repeatedly order the Muslims to kill the Infidels *(Non-Muslims)* wherever they *(Muslims)* found us *(Infidels)?*

The Quran is redundant in saying that there is only one God – Allah. I happen to feel that Yahweh is a better entry, in that He represents Love and Peace; whereas, Allah is very combative and is to be feared.

Is it because the author is not Allah or the Angel Gabriel, but, perhaps, Muhammad instead?

What disturbs me is that there are over a thousand pages in the Quran. And, I ask myself:

'Did the Angel Gabriel really give Muhammad the Quran?

I am challenged in the Quran to produce one chapter that could match what was written if I don't believe that it was written by Allah.

Would I be able to write the Quran, as challenged, if I could proclaim myself a Prophet?'

As redundant as the Quran is with the threats of the Scourge for Infidels, the streams flowing in Paradise, the dark-eyed virgins that will be given to the Believers *(dead Muslims),* mentioning Noah, Abraham, Lot, the Pharoah and Moses, David, Bathsheba, Solomon, then bashing Jesus, and reminding the readers about Sodom and Gemorrah, I think I can I only have to write 200 pages and repeat myself often.

I also believe that Yahweh and Allah are not the same God, as evidenced by my opening statement. My God asks a lot of me in the Bible, but never to take a man's life just because he disagrees with me about the Bible. No!

Bible vs Quran

Believers - Muslims

(Reference Suras 3:100, 3:118, 3:149, 4:91, 4:92, 23:1, 60:10)

The Quran is encouraging Muslims to isolate themselves from the Unbelievers *(the rest of the world)* in order to ensure that they remain true to their faith.

Why is it so important that a Muslim surrounds himself only with other Muslims? Why is the Quran so insecure that a Muslim cannot have a social life?

If Allah were as powerful, merciful and forgiving as the Quran makes him out to be, why shouldn't a Muslim meet other people and learn about life away from his faith?

Why would the Quran give a Muslim the authority to kill someone who doesn't believe in Islam?

This is a part of life; meeting people and talking about various subjects of interest. If the subject happens to be religion, and the friend is sincerely trying to make a point about differences in opinion, is it necessary that he be destroyed? As in killed?

The Quran says that if a Muslim kills another Muslim accidentally, he must surrender *one Muslim slave* and pay blood money to the family of the victim, or, if he chooses, he can give it in alms *(like tithes – to the church).*

Why is Islam still practicing slavery? How did Islam bring slavery into America? We have had racial problems which started with slavery, then graduated to segregation, and now, people who refuse to accept the changes of today. Yet, Islam can practice slavery?

The Quran states that if a believing woman *(in the Islamic faith)* seeks refuge with a Muslim man, he should test her belief. If she is a true believer, do not return her to the Infidels for they are not lawful for them.

Her status is that of a slave *unless he provides her with a dowry and marries her. Why would a woman consent to this type of relationship?*

A believer is blessed who is humble in his prayers; who avoids profane talk, and give alms to the destitute; who restrain their carnal desires *(except with their wives and **slave girls**)* for these are lawful to them; who are true to their trusts and promises, and diligent in their prayers. They shall abide in Paradise forever.

The disturbing parts are the slave girls and abiding in Paradise forever. The comment about slave girls is contained in **Slaves**. See **Paradise** regarding abiding there forever.

Here, again, this is supposed to be a Religion?

Jesus, Son of Mary

(Reference Suras 2:233, 3:46, 4:155, 4:171, 10:68, 17:111, 19:17, 19:27, 57:27)

The Quran is challenging the Bible about the status of Jesus. They are claiming that Jesus was not a Messiah, but an Apostle appointed by Allah.

The Quran also chastise the Christians for denying the truth; that Jesus was put to death by Allah. He was not crucified. The Christians thought he was. But that was not true.

Christians say that 'God has begotten a son.' The Quran challenges that by saying, 'God forbid! Self-sufficient is He. His is all that the heavens and the earth contain.'

In **Sura 19:18**, the Quran claims that Allah sent His spirit in the semblance of a man who said to Mary: 'I am but your Lord's emissary, and have come to give you a holy son.'

Mary said, 'How shall I bear a child when I have neither been touched by any man nor ever been unchaste?'

'Thus did your Lord speak,' he replied, 'That is easy enough for Me. He shall be a sign to mankind and a blessing from Us. This is Our decree.'

Thereupon she conceived him, and retired to a far-off place. And when she felt the throes of childbirth, she lay down by the trunk of a palm tree, crying: 'Oh, would that I had died before this, and passed into oblivion!'

The Quran bypassed the Manger Scene and the Three Kings who traveled from afar. Does it matter who's right or who's wrong? The answer is: it matters when it is reported by three of Jesus' Disciples of the occurrence in the Bible versus a lone author in the Quran.

Then in **Sura 19:30**, the Quran continues: Carrying the child, she came to her people, who said to her: 'Mary, this is indeed a strange thing! Your father was never a whoremonger, nor was your mother a harlot.'

Mary made a sign to them, pointing to the child. But, they replied: 'How can we speak with a babe in the cradle?'

Whereupon Jesus spoke *(See the Sura 19:30 and Chapter 3) I don't recall Jesus speaking as a Babe in the Bible, and I've read the Bible a number of times. Did I miss something?*

Such was Jesus, son of Mary. That is the whole truth, which the Christians still doubt. God forbid that He Himself should beget a son! When He decrees a thing, He need only say: 'Be,' and it is.

The Quran continues that Allah bestowed prophethood to the offsprings of Noah and Abraham. Some were rightly guided, but many were evil-doers. After them Allah sent other apostles, and after those, Jesus, the son of Mary.

Finally, the Quran says: 'Believers, have fear of Allah and put your trust in His apostle, Muhammad, who will grant you double share of His mercy.

I will refrain from comment here. I find it difficult to believe and will comment at the end.

Jews and Christians (Unbelievers – Infidels)

(Reference Suras 2:113, 2:166, 3:19, 5:14, 8:12, 9:30, 98:6)

In these Suras, the author attempts to dissuade the reader from the

Jews and Christians, and suggests that Allah said that Islam is the only true faith.

Allah claims to have made a covenant with the Jews, but they broke it. The same applied to the Christians. Therefore, Allah stirred hatred between the Jews and Christians.

Here is another part that I have difficulty in believing. Allah revealed His will to the angels, saying: 'I shall be with you. Give courage to the believers. I shall cast terror into the hearts of the Infidels, Strike off their heads, strike off the very tips of their fingers.

The brutality in this Sura is frightening. I would challenge, not only the audacity of Allah demanding His followers to strike off the heads of Infidels, but question the doctrine on which this Religion was founded.

Let me be clear. Is this a Religion?

Now that I am aware of what is being said of me and other Christians in the Quran, I'm hurt. I feel violated because Muslims are being told that the People of the Book (Christians) shall burn forever in the fire of Hell; we are the vilest of all creatures.

Life On Earth vs. Life After

(Reference Suras 9:38, 14:3, 17:9, 44:51)

I gave you four Suras that glorify the life to come over this life on earth. Throughout the Quran, the hints of the magnificence of the life after are astounding.

Is it any wonder that the Arab countries have no problems in recruiting Suicide Bombers? I consider these passages dangerous. They *(Suras)* are advocating leaving this life for a better place, and at the same time, in Sura 4:29, Allah says, 'Do not kill each other.'

The suicide rate for Muslims in Los Angeles is reported as being up by 15.5%. (InFocus News April 2009). The reason for the increase is not clear.

I'm not a "Shrink" but I would guess that these Suras and the Suras on Paradise (below) contribute a lot to the increase in numbers of Muslim suicides.

Make War

(Reference Suras 9:14, 9:123, 47:4)

Allah is a combat field commander rallying his troops, the Believers, to Make War on the Infidels who dwell around them.

Muhammad – Jesus Claims Muhammad Will Follow Him?

(Reference Suras 61:6, 8:65, 35:30, 48:1, 48:29, 53:1)

The Quran repeatedly bash the Jews and Christians of not telling the truth.

In Sura 53:1, the Quran, referring to Muhammad, states: 'His own heart did not deny his vision. How can you question what he sees?'

If this is factual, is the author of the Quran on a guilt trip? Why wouldn't I believe it if I were a Muslim reading the Book of my Religion?

On a footnote of Sura 66:1, it states: 'Muhammad, We* are told, was once found by his wife, Hafsah, with a Coptic Slave from whom he had promised her to separate. Of this Hafsah secretly informed 'A'ishah, another wife of his, To free Muhammad from his promise to Hafsah was the object of this chapter. Some of the references are obscure.

*We is supposed to imply that Allah and Gabriel are talking. I find this rather strange. Didn't Allah know about Muhammad's wives?

What does "Some of the references are obscure" mean? Isn't Allah supposed to know everything? Why did they even bother putting this footnote in the Quran?

Muslims

(Reference Suras 5:3, 5:6, 8:16, 72:14)

I would not be a good Muslim. If my God threatened me with the Scourge and to burn me in Hell as fuel for the fire, I would say, "No you won't!" Then, I would go find me a loving God.

Yes! My God is the God of Love and Peace.

Paradise – Virgins – The Garden of Eden (for Believers)

(Reference Suras 18:30, 22:23, 35:31, 37:40, 38:50, 43:70, 47:12, 52:15, 55:52, 55:67, 56:1)

All through the Quran, the author glorifies the presence of Paradise – in the world to come. There is hardly a chapter that doesn't mention or hints of Paradise.

The beauty and fantasy of Paradise with dark-eyed virgins waiting on you, ready to serve whatever it is you desire, puts this fairyland in the forefront of your mind.

Is it any wonder that the Arabs have no problems in recruiting Suicide Bombers?

What are our chances of bringing Democracy to the Mid-east when it is populated by mindless robots who acknowledge this Paradise? We would have to change the mindset of the country.

Quran (Koran)

(Reference Suras 10:34, 11:13, 20:113, 21:5, 22:16, 27:1)

The author attempts to persuade us that the Quran could not have been devised by any but God. "It confirms what was revealed before it and fully explains the Scriptures. It is beyond doubt from the Lord of the Universe."

If we say that the Quran was written by Muhammad, it dares us to produce ten chapters like it. I think I can do that.

In the author's defense, from the introductions I have read, the Quran is very poetic with captivating prose that would tax the minds of mortal men. Therefore, my Challenges on the three Qurans I have read are at the mercy of the brilliance of translators.

But, according to Sura 27:1, it is "a guide and joyful tidings to true believers, who attend to their prayers and render the alms levy and firmly believe in the life to come."

I guess I'll have to wait until I get to the next level – "the life to come."

Sabbath

(Reference Sura 16:124)

The Sabbath was ordained only for those who differed about it. On the Day of Resurrection your Lord will judge their disputes.

I didn't think there was any dispute about the Sabbath Day. Why do I have to wait until the Day of Resurrection to find out what day it falls on? The Bible tells of the Sabbath Day in many passages. However, through the years, many scholars have come up with their own interpretations as to when it is supposed to be. I trust that we have the right answers in Chapter 4.

Slaves

(Reference Suras 4:36, 23:1, 24:31, 34:32, 58:3)

There are many chapters that mention female slaves, slave girls, free a slave in the Quran. I found five Suras that you could use for your interpretation.

In the Sura that Allah made lawful to Muhammad to have slave girls "whom Allah has given you as booty," it demeans the female role in life. I think that every girl should be up in arms over this.

Unbelievers (Infidels) –To Hell – The Fire – The Scourge

(Reference Suras 2:24, 2:89, 2:126, 3:4, 3:10, 3:116, 4:89, 7:35, 87:10)

This is the category where you and I fall into.

We are threatened all through the Quran with the scourge of the fire, going to Hell, being used as fuel for the fire and promised an evil fate.

So, for us, we will be heirs of the fire, wherein we shall abide forever.

Women Of Islam

(Reference Suras 2:222, 2:228, 4:3, 4:11, 4:34)

As evidenced by the Suras mentioned above and in the Quran, Allah doesn't give much credit to the women of Islam. I have already beaten that subject into the ground, so I'll let up.

Jesus vs Muhammad

Miracles

In the introduction of the Quran, a comment was made that Muhammad did not perform any miracles. I wondered about that.

Why did Allah think that it was not necessary that Muhammad performed any miracles?

Since Allah chose Muhammad to be a Prophet and Islam to be the Religion of the Muslims, how was Muhammad supposed to compete with the image of Jesus?

Sura 61:6

And recall when Jesus, son of Mary, said: 'O children of Israel! Verily I am Allah's Messenger to you, confirming the Torah before me and conveying the glad news of a Messenger coming after me; his name will be Ahmad.

Then when he came to them with evidence, they said: 'This is manifest magic.'

America vs. Islam

I was going to use a cartoon here that showed a Teacher in the front of her classroom with a combat veteran in a wheel chair. All the children are standing, except one, with their hands over their heart about to recite the Pledge of Allegiance.

The Teacher says to the lad that is sitting:"Kevin, it's your right not to stand for the Pledge . . . but, let me introduce you to someone who can't stand because he was defending that right."

I regret that I could not find the name of the artist.

Only 31 Words

I PLEDGE ALLEGIANCE TO THE FLAG OF THE UNITED STATES OF AMERICA, AND TO THE REPUBLIC FOR WHICH IT STANDS, ONE NATION UNDER GOD, INDIVISIBLE, WITH LIBERTY AND JUSTICE FOR ALL.

Isn't Life Strange?

The next photo showed a military veteran overlooking a cemetery with a caption that read:

"I Never Met One Veteran Who Enlisted To Fight For Socialism."

Let Us Pray

The next cartoon shows a mother and her two children at the dinner table about to say grace.

The caption below the cartoon reads:

"If Muslims can pray on Madison Avenue, why are Christians banned from praying in public and erecting religious displays on their holy days?"

I believe it's time we stand up for what we believe!

Beheading

"Allah revealed His will to the angels, saying: 'I shall be with you. Give courage to the believers. I shall cast terror into the hearts of the infidels. *Strike off their heads*, strike off the very tips of their fingers!' (Sura 8:12)

This is barbaric. It is not believable that Allah would proclaim the destruction of his children by beheading. And, if the Muslims wish to continue in their Islamic Faith with this ideology in their Quran, then this is proof enough that they should be removed from America.

Paradise

Can anyone prove what was said about Paradise?

If Allah wrote the Quran, I guess He could describe anything He pleases about Paradise being what He says it is. But, I have a problem with that.

Why would He want to portray Paradise as being such a glorious place to be when the "less than normal" people would consider suicide as a way to end their misery here on earth for it?

I can't help but think that Al Qaeda has little trouble recruiting for Suicide Bombers because of this passage in the Quran.

This is another reason that Islam needs to be driven out of America. Their doctrine is a hazard to the safety of the people of America.

Four Wives

Did Allah permit the male Muslims four wives, or was it Muhammad?

The answer is not important. It's the doctrine that is faulty. It is the doctrine that would tempt the down-trodden males to opt out of Christianity for a shot at a better life with Islam.

Is this a tool to encourage membership in Islam? How shameful!

Women's Role

Do you think it's fair that Allah made the Muslim male superior to Muslim women?

It's written all over the Quran. No wonder the Muslim males don't want their wives to get an education. If the women could read, why would they want to stay a Muslim?

Can you imagine a Representative introducing legislation on the Floor suggesting that each American male be allowed to have four wives? He would be laughed off the Floor.

Life After

Are you content with this life in preference to the life to come? Few are the blessings of this life, compared with those of the life to come. (Sura 9: 38)

As for the righteous, they shall be lodged in peace together amid gardens and fountains, arrayed in rich silks and fine brocade. Even thus; and We shall wed them to dark-eyed houris. Secure against all ills, they shall call for every kind of fruit; and, having died once, they shall die no more. (Sura 44:49)

This subject is very troubling to me because of the number of suicides recorded on Muslims in America. It doesn't take a 'rocket scientist' to figure out the reason for the high numbers that would commit suicide. Couple that with temptations that Al-Qaeda offers for suicide bombers, and you've got serious problems brewing on a continuing basis.

I can't believe that Allah would describe the 'Life After' so eloquently. Granted, He made it clear that the Believer had to do good deeds (one of which is to destroy Infidels), behaving in accordance with the Quran. But, the 'Life After' is very tempting for the down-trodden.

For this reason, I challenge the authenticity of the Quran being written by Allah. I honestly feel that Muhammad wrote it.

Throughout the Quran, the question is asked, "Can you write one chapter of the Quran?"

I would answer that question very sarcastically, YES! I can write the whole Quran. And, I can write it better than Muhammad did – and, I don't have to be as redundant as he was.

Jihad

This trouble maker was added as the sixth Pillar The doctrine of jihad has been invoked to justify wars between Muslim and non-Muslim states and even to legitimate wars between Muslims themselves. Adversaries would be branded as heretics or rebels to warrant the application of the jihad doctrine. In the 18th and 19th centuries, they were often referred to as jihad movements.

Despite their geographical range – from West Africa to Southeast Asia – and the different social, economic, and political causes from which they sprang, they employed the same notions from the Islamic repertoire. Jihad, for them meant the struggle within an only nominally Islamic society for the purification of religion and the establishment of a genuine Islamic community.

Israel vs. Islam

Population

The Global Islamic population is approximately 1,200,000,000; that is One Billion, Two Hundred Million or twenty (20%) percent of the world/s population.

They have received the following Nobel Prizes: (Total 7)

Literature	Peace	Economics	Physics	Medicine
1988 Najib Mahfooz	1978 Anwar El Sadat 1990 Elias Corey 1994 Yaser Arafat 1999 Ahmed Zewai	None	None	1960 Peter Medawar 1998 Ferid Mourad

The Global Jewish population is approximately 14,000,000; that is Fourteen Million or about two-hundredths (0.02%) of one percent of the world's population

They have received the following Nobel Prizes: (Total 129)

Literature	Peace	Economics	Physics	*Medicine*
1910 Paul Heyse	1911 Alfred Fried	1970 Paul Samuelson	1905 Adolph Baeyer	1908 ElieMetchnikoff
1927 Henri Bergson	1911 Tobias Asser	1971 Simon Kuznets	1906 Henri Moissan	1908 Paul Erlich
1958 BorisPasternak	1968 Rene Cassin	1972 Kenneth Arrow	1907 Alb Michelson	1914 Robert Barany
1966 Shmuel Agnon	1973 H. Kissinger	1975 LeonidKantorovich	1908 GabeLippmann	1922 Otto Meyerhof
1966 Nelly Sachs	1978 MenacheBegin	1976 Milton Friedman	1910 Otto Wallach	1936 Ottto Loewi
1976 Saul Bellow	1986 Elie Wiesel	1978 Herbert Simon	1915 RicWillstaetter	1944 Joseph Erlanger
1978 Isaac Singer	1994 Shimon :Peres	1980 Lawrence Klein	1918 Fritz Haber	1944 Herbert Gasser
1981 Elias Canetti	1994 Yitzhak Rabin	1985 Franco Modigliani	1921 Albert Einstein	1945 Ernst Chain
1987 Joseph Brodsky		1987 Robert Solow	1922 Niels Bohr	1946 HermannMuller
1991 Nad Gordimer		1990 Harry Markowitz	1925 JamesFranck	1950 Tade Reichstein
		1992 Gary Becker	1925 Gustav Hertz	1952 Selm Waksman
		1993 Robert Fogel	1943 Gustav Stern	1953 Hans Krebs
			1944 Isidor Rabi	1953 Fritz Lipmann
			1952 Felix Bloch	1958 Josh Lederberg
			1954 Max Born	1959 ArthurKornberg
			1958 Igor Tamm	1964 Konrad Bloch
			1959 Emilio Segre	1965 Andre Lwoff

Literature	Peace	Economics	Physics	*Medicine*
			1960 Donald Glaser	1967 George Wald
			1961 Rob Hofstadter	1968 MarshNirenberg
			1961 Melvin Calvin	1969 Salvador Luria
			1962 Lev Landau	1970 Julius Axelrod Sir BernardKatz
			1962 Max Perutz	1972 Gerald Edelman
			1965 Rich Feynman	1975 Howard Temin
			1965 JuliaSchwinger	1976 BaruchBlumberg
			1969 Mu Gell-Mann	1977 Howard Temin
			1971 Dennis Gabor	1978 Daniel Nathans
			1972 William Stein	1980 Baruj Cerraf
			1973 DaveJosephson	1984 Cesar Milstein
			1975 Ben Mottleson	1985 Michael Brown
			1976 Burton Richter	1985 Joseph Goldstein
			1977 Ilya Prigogine	1986 Stanley Cohen
			1978 Arno Penzias	1986 Rita Montalcinij
			1978 Peter Kapitza	1988 Gertrude Elion
			1979 SteveWeinberg	1989 Harold Varmus
			1979 Sheld Glashow	1991 Erwin Neher
			1979 Herbert Brown	1991 Bert Sakmann

Literature	Peace	Economics	Physics	*Medicine*
			1980 Paul Berg	1993 Richard Roberts
			1980 Walter Gilbert	1993 Phillip Sharp
			1981 RoalHoffmann	1994 Alfred Gilman
			1982 Aaron King	1995 Edward Lewis
			1985 AlbeHauptman	1996 LuRose Iacovino
			1985 Jerome Karle	
			1986 Du Herschbach	
			1988 Robert Huber	
			1988 Leon Lederman	
			1988 Melvi Schwartz	
			1988 Jac Steinberger	
			1989 Sidney Altman	
			1990 JeromeFriedman	
			1992 Rudolp Marcus	
			1995 Martin Perl	
			2000 Alan Heeger	

Differences

The Jews are NOT promoting brain washing children in military training camps, teaching them how to blow themselves up and cause maximum deaths of Jews and other non-Muslims.

The Jews don't hijack planes, nor kill athletes at the Olympics, or blow themselves up in German restaurants.

There is NOT one single Jew who has destroyed a church.

There is NOT one single Jew who protests by killing people.

The Jews don't traffic slaves, nor have leaders calling for Jihad and death to all the Infidels *(Non-Believers of the Muslim faith).*

Considerations

Perhaps the world's Muslims should consider investing more in standard education and less in blaming the Jews for all their problems.

Muslims must ask 'what can they do for humankind' before they demand that humankind respect them.

Regardless of your feelings about the crisis between Israel and the Palestinians and Arab neighbors, even if you believe there is more culpability on Israel's part, the following two sentences really say it all:

'If the Arabs put down their weapons today, there would be no more violence.

'If the Jews put down their weapons today, there would be no more Israel.'

– *Benjamin Netanyahu*

General Eisenhower Warned Us

It is a matter of history that when the Supreme Commander of the Allied Forces, General Dwight Eisenhower, found the victims of the death camps, he ordered all possible photographs to be taken, and for the German people from surrounding villages to be ushered through the camps and even made to bury the dead.

He did this because he said in words to this effect:

'Get it all on record now – get the films – get the witnesses because somewhere down the road of history, some bastard will get up and say that this never happened.'

Comments

Recently, the UK debated whether to remove The Holocaust from its school curriculum because it 'offends' the Muslim population which claims it never occurred.

It is not removed as yet. However, this is a frightening portent of the fear that is gripping the world and how easily each country is giving in to it.

It is now more than 60 years after the Second World War in Europe ended.

In memory of the 6 million Jews, 20 million Russians, 10 million Christians, and 1,900 Catholic priests who were 'murdered, raped, burned, starved, beaten, experimented on and humiliated' while the German people looked the other way.

Now, more than ever, with Iran, among others, claiming the Holocaust to be 'a myth,' it is imperative to make sure the world never forgets.

How many years will it be before the attack on the World Trade Center 'Never Happened' because it offends some Muslim in the United States?

SUMMARY

I have heard the arguments in comparing the Quran to the Bible. But, the point to take into consideration is 'verification of the truth.'

Each book in the Bible has an author, not necessarily the same. But, the facts and the substances are.

The Quran, on the other hand, was authored by a lone author – pick one: Allah, the Angel Gabriel or Muhammad.

The Quran claims that it was written by Allah. The point is that we're taking the word of the lone author of the Quran vs. many authors of the Bible.

All through the Quran, the author states that Allah was not pleased with the Jews because they did not believe in all that He said and told them that the Devil distracted them. So Allah sent Jesus to guide the Jews back on the right path. But, here again, Christianity was formed and the Jews did not follow that thought. The Devil created a division between the two sects.

Then, Allah sent the Angel Gabriel to Muhammad to introduce Islam to unite the people of His Kingdom. He knew that temptations would be used by the Devil, so Allah had Rashad and Ahmad held in the wings to be interjected as necessary.

In the article "European Life Died In Auschwitz," it is a sad commentary of the holocaust, which most of Islam refuse to accept happened. But, the anger of the author of what had happened to Europe can be felt.

If I were to believe what was proclaimed above, would I be declared the DEVIL, an Unbeliever and must be killed? Also, by saying that Islam is violating every code of common decency of humankind and must be stopped, am I subjecting myself to the sword?

We have enough problems with securing our borders and guarding ourselves against terrorism. Islam represents terrorism from within our borders.

Here's the scary part, Folks! This Administration is not going to do a thing about this problem. Is it because they are a part of the problem?

We may have to take things into our own hands and forcibly remove Islam.

The next Summary is on Page 146. However, we urge you to read the rest of the book. Our case is made stronger and the rest of the pages reveal facts that will scare you out of your wits, so that as we get closer to the end and our final conclusion, you will agree with our summation that Islam must be forced out of America.

Chapter 10
Show Islam The Way Out

Preparation

In Chapter 8, we learned from an expert who lived and worked in Saudi Arabia for 20 years, that *A Good Muslim Cannot Be A Good American*. The reasons he gave are in keeping with the way Muslims are taught from the Quran and the Madrassas, the schools.

With that as a starting point, our task is not going to be an easy one. We don't have the time to re-train the Muslim minds into accepting our way of life over theirs. So, we begin our task.

The Easy Way

If I were President, this would be a simple situation to overcome. I would form a Council of Church Leaders with a mission: "to define a religion." If Islam does not meet with the definition of a religion, as I suspect it would not, *(because Allah is filled with Hatred)* then with the powers vested in my Administration, the Congress and Senate, Islam would be removed from the borders of the United States of America.

The Hard Way

Since we have no power, and since the President is Pro-Islam, we will have to do it the hard way. We will have to rally the support of the people through the Tea Party, like we did in the 2010 Election, only this time with a little more gusto, and focus on the Mission Statement.

Tea Partiers

You are the key to the success of this plan. A copy of this book was sent to the Tea Party Newsletter Headquarters.

Become a part of the plan - Jump on board! Get a book! Tell all your friends about this book and our plan to reclaim our America.

Assumptions:

That the President and his Administration will not assist us in our mission statement. With the facts staring them in the face, they are still unaware of the Origin of Terrorism;

That the media will try to discredit us from the outset because of their radical leanings against what is right. It is such a shame that the media chose to identify with the liberals, rather than being neutral. When our mission is achieved, our slogan, "Be American or Be Gone" will also apply to the Media, as well.

That we will have to rally our forces to exercise our right of Free Speech to oppose Islam in the United States;

That we can count on the Patriots, the Tea Party, the Christians, Jews, other religions, and the Veterans, who have already paid a price for their services, to rally behind us in our effort to overcome the evil forces of Islam;

That we can, hopefully, influence the countries of Canada, Mexico and Central America to join us in our crusade to make North America Islam Free;

That we can ask Australia to help us as we encourage the European countries, the South American countries, Asian countries and friendly African countries we can find, to help us;

That there are still countries with more natives than Muslims. They can help their cause by joining forces with us while they can before they are overrun by Muslims. We would encourage them to read the paragraph on helping us as "Country Donors;" and,

That our mission also includes "Getting Active Politically To Vote for a new Administration" to rid us of the faulty policies that makes America look weak to the world - And, get rid of them for bankrupting the US.

Mission Statement To Eliminate Islam

Step 1: Stop Islam from doing anything in the United States until such time as they rewrite their political and religious doctrine to eliminate the terror threats, and learn to preach love and peace, as do the Torah and the Bible.

Step 2:   If Islam cannot comply with Step 1, Islam is to Cease and Desist from doing anything in the United States until they can prove beyond a reasonable doubt that they are not a Terrorist Organization. That will be difficult for them to do without rewriting the Quran and disassociating themselves from Saudi Arabia.

Step 3:   If Islam cannot comply with Step 1 and / or Step 2, then rally the Tea Party to demonstrate against what we believe is "Terrorism Within Our Borders" to let Islam know that we are very aware of their faulty doctrine whether they care to admit it or not, and we will rally until our government gets involved to take appropriate actions

Step 4:   Rally with placards to stop the purchase of gas from OPEC countries. Buy only oil products from America. This will start a gas war to lower the cost of gas. Never Give Up! Pray, that in time, *the people of America will vote this Party out of office and elect a President with Gonads to secure our borders and our country against the likes of Islam or any other "take over" cults.*

Business Opportunities

Included here were all the things that were related to this chapter that I thought would be ideal business opportunities to put America back to work. But, after pages and pages of "Things To Do," it appeared that I would have to form a Company to accomplish all that was suggested.

I'm too old to undertake another business venture. So, I think that the best thing to do is to turn it over to the Tea Party. Tea Partiers: If you are interested in promoting businesses for your members, I can help in an advisory capacity.

Overview (Our "To Do" List)

Circulate This Book
Stop Purchasing Gas From OPEC - Promote US Oil Companies
Force the Enemy Out Now! Rally the Tea Party – Display placards

Circulation

Ask your friends to go on-line to www.onguardamerica.com. Get a book. Included in the price are Updates to the GOP Candidates and their progression in the polls. The Updates will be e-mailed monthly until we get the President out of office, or Election Day November 2012.

Country Donors: For countries who are concerned about the number of Muslims within your borders, who wish to move toward democracy, email our Director of Operations (www.onguardamerica.org) and Thank You in advance. We will ensure that your contribution is put in the hands of the new Administration. We will work harder to take the White House so that we can help you with your borders.

Every one of the 1.2 billion Muslims in the world need a copy of this book to see the flaws of the Quran and how to overcome their problems.

Autographed Copies Of This Book

Since I cannot make personal appearances until we force Islam out of America, I will not be able to schedule Book Signing Events anywhere.

I need to get this book circulated so that everyone in America will be informed about what is taking place in the political arena – especially, how we intend to remove the President from office before 2012.

Tea Partiers: I need your help:
1. To circulate this book; and,
2. To encourage requests for autographed copies of the book.

Circulation: If you can ask your friends to get a copy of this book, and everyone does the same thing, the Conservatives all over America will be informed in a relatively short period of time.

Autographed Copies: Go to www.onguardamerica.org and purchase five books from Authorhouse.com, then fill out the bottom of the form (name, address, email, etc), and submit your request. I will mail you an autographed copy of the book and a note of (*Mahalo*) appreciation.

You can give the five books to your family or friends. If anything happens to me, you will have a treasure – double your investment.

A Chance To Meet: When we force Obama out of office, we will ask former Governor and Vice-Presidential Candidate Sarah Palin and Congresswoman and Presidential Hopeful Michelle Bachmann to arrange a time and place to gather so we can thank you for your help.

New Christmas Song

Have you heard the new Christmas song?

When we take the White House, we will be in time to decorate the place with a huge Christmas Tree. Then, we can gather around to sing carols and the new Christmas Song.

The lyrics are great. Brilliant job!

New Christmas Song

I believe in Christmas   *I believe it's true*

I believe our Savior   *Was sent here for me and you*

If you believe in Christmas   *Join us in this song*

Keep saying "Merry Christmas"   *And keep that spirit all year long*

If you don't see Merry Xmas in the window, No you don't go in that store
If you don't see Merry Xmas in the window, Yes you walk right by that door
Oh, it's all about the little baby Jesus, It's my savior's day of birth
It's the one and only reason that we celebrate the season
Wishing love and peace to all upon the earth

If you don't hear Merry Xmas when they greet you, When you're walking through that store
Simply turn and say "It's nice to meet you!" As you walk right out that door
Words are chosen every year to hide it's Xmas, the reason for our holiday
They're not happy what you're singin', but they want their tills a ringin'
Try'na sell my Christmas every other way
Come and stand out from the crowd, Say Merry Christmas and be proud
Christmas isn't just another day

NARRATIVE:

What would be missing? Now let's see, if not for Christ's Nativity
No Silent Night or First Noels, No Santa's sleigh or jingle bells
No star atop the Xmas tree, No special day for family
No bells that ring for angel's wings, No dolls and trains that Santa brings
No drummer boys or Tiny Tim, No Mr. Scrooge – we all know him
No list of who's been good or bad, Well, maybe, that won't be too sad
No candy canes or mistletoes, No Christmas lights out in the snow
No stockings hung with so much care, Hoping Santa finds them there
And, one more thing that wouldn't be, No- ooo partridge in a pear – Rump a bum bum

If you don't see Merry Xmas in the window, No you don't go in that store
If you don't see Merry Xmas in the window, Yes you walk right by that door
If you don't believe the reason for my Xmas, Then it's sure okay with me
Please don't tell me what to sing or what music I can play
After all my Christmas is my special day

*Come and stand out from the crowd, Say Merry Christmas and be proud
Christmas isn't just another holiday*

MERRY CHRISTMAS

No More

In the previous chapters, I have presented my case, and Challenged Islam with their Quran and the facts about Wahhabism and Jihad.

In this chapter, I am asking your help to Show Islam The Way Out:

NO MORE Mosques; NO MORE Blocking Roadways While Muslims Pray; NO MORE Sharia Law; NO MORE No Profiling; NO MORE No Christmas; NO MORE No Manger Scenes; NO MORE Try Not To Offend Islam; NO MORE Burkas and Veils in Airports; NO MORE ISLAM.

Arabian Faith

I have many friends who converted to Islam because of the racial issues that have been going on far too long in America. Would they have converted if there were other outlets whereby they could vent their frustrations?

We have formed an organization especially for Arab Americans who were former Muslims who are more concerned about remaining in America than they are in the doctrines of Islam.

We encourage Muslims who are willing to turn away from the harsh doctrine of the Quran to become members of the Arabian Faith.

Wahhabism encourages Muslims to slay those who step away from Islam because they have become Infidels. The band of Arabian Faith, with the help of local law enforcement, will protect them from harm.

As we rally our forces to Show Islam the way out of America, we will welcome members to the Arabian Faith, to the circle of Religions of the World, who can coexist in America.

Members must learn the Pledge of Allegiance and We The People. It will be well worth it. Welcome aboard!

As the membership grows, we will identify qualified personnel who would be interested in forming a staff to help organize and operate the Arabian Faith. If you have any questions, feel free to email us at arabianfaith@teamoga.com.

With Gas Prices On The Rise – Let's Start A Gas War!

All the major oil companies purchase their gas from Saudi Arabia or OPEC.

Are you aware that the Saudis are boycotting American products? In addition, they are gouging us on oil prices. Shouldn't we return the favor?

Can't we take control of our own destiny and let these giant oil importers know who REALLY generates their profits, their LIFESTYLE?

How about leaving American Dollars in America and reduce the import/export deficit?

Let's STOP buying oil products from **Shell, Chevron, Texaco, Exxon, Marathon, Mobil, Speedway, Amoco and Citgo.** All purchase their products from Saudi Arabia. Citgo is Hugo Chavez's Oil Company.

An appealing remedy might be to boycott their GAS. Every time you fill up your car you can avoid putting more money into the coffers of Saudi Arabia.

If we can purchase gas only from American owned and operated Gas Companies, we can make an impact by choking off the cash flow to Saudi Arabia. Over a period of time, they will feel the pain.

Hugo Chavez is changing the name of his gas stations because he is already feeling the pain from declining sales.

Our dollar may be in trouble, but our Purchasing Power is still King. Money Talks!

Purchase gas from companies that don't import oil from the Saudis.

Nothing is more frustrating than the feeling that every time I fill up my tank, I'm sending my money to people who I get the impression want me, my family and my friends dead. The following gas companies import Middle Eastern oil:

Shell	205,742,000 barrels
Chevron/Texaco	144,332,000 barrels
Exxon /Mobil	130,082,000 barrels
Marathon/Speedway	117,740,000 barrels
Amoco	62,231,000 barrels

And CITGO oil is imported from Venezuela by Dictator Hugo Chavez who hates America and openly avows our economic destruction! *(We pay Chavez's regime nearly $10 Billion per year in oil revenues!)*

The U.S. imports 5,517,000 barrels of crude oil per day from OPEC.

If you do the math at $100 per barrel, that's over $550 million per DAY *($200 BILLION per YEAR!)* handed over to OPEC, many of whose members are our confirmed enemies!

It won't stop here - oil prices could go to $200 a barrel or higher if we keep buying from them.

Where To Buy American Gasoline.

Here are some large companies that do not import Middle Eastern oil:

Sunoco	0 barrels
Conoco	0 barrels
0 A Sinclair	0 barrels
BP / Phillips	0 barrels
Hess	0 barrels
ARC0	0 barrels
Maverick	0 barrels
Flying J	0 barrels
Valero	0 barrels
Murphy Oil USA*	0 barrels

*Sold at WalMart, gas is from South Arkansas and fully USA owned and produced.

*Not only that but they give scholarships to all children in their town who finish high school and are legal US citizens.

All of this information is available from the U.S. Department of Energy and each company is required to state where they get their oil and how much they are importing.

But to have a real impact, we need to reach literally millions of gas buyers. Get on your email list of friends and tell them about this. Better still, tell them to get a copy of this book.

Mom and Pop Gas Stations

If you are a franchise gas station purchasing your gas from OPEC Oil Companies, we're sorry for the inconvenience we may be causing you.

We can help you with oil products from one of the American Oil Companies. Please let us know if we can help you.

Please understand that the sooner we can stop the flow of cash to Saudi Arabia and their terror organizations controlling oil products, the sooner we will be able to take control of our American destiny.

Placards

We have a few ideas for placards that can be made for the Tea Party to help spread the word of what we are trying to do. Below are a few samples.

Tea Partiers: we welcome your thoughts

Advertising From Personal Autos and Vans

Tea Partiers: Consider having Gasoline Ad Placards to fit on your automobile advertising "Where To Buy Gas" and 'Where Not To Buy Gas." Send a picture of your car to the Tea Party Headquarters. They can probably work out some entitlement for you that can turn into cash credits.

Delta Airlines

Now we learn that Delta Airlines has co-opted with Saudi Arabian Airlines for travel to the Mid-East.

Should we add placards opposing their decision and rally against their partnership with the Enemy?

I have already cut my Delta – American Express Card in half. Now, I will have to find an Airline Company that I can call my Air Carrier. And, on the card, there are enough of them out there. I'll wait for an offer.

ISLAM Is not a Religion **They are** TERRORISTS	**HELP US** Drive Out The Evil Forces Of **ISLAM**	Buy American Gasoline Not Gasoline **FROM OPEC**
CUT OFF THE **CASH FLOW TO** **SAUDI ARABIA** **BUY GAS FROM** **U.S. OIL CO'S.**	**ROAST PORK** **DINNER** $5.00 Per Person **MUSLIMS FREE**	**ISLAM** Promotes Terror Learn The Truth About The **EVIL EMPIRE**
Islam Hates **Homosexuals** **Help Us Drive** **Them Out**	**FOR SALE** **PIG THYROID** **FERTILIZER** **$5.00 / BAG**	**BE AMERICAN** **OR** **BE GONE**
BECOME AN **INFIDEL** **Before It Is** **TOO LATE**	**You don't have** **to go to** **Paradise.** **HAWAII**	**MUSLIM WOMEN** **BE AMERICAN** **DRESS WESTERN**
BE AN **Arabian** **Knight** **DRESS WESTERN**	**You don't have** **to die to go to** **Paradise.** **TAHITI**	**BECOME AN** **INFIDEL** **To Stay In** **AMERICA**

You don't have to die to go to Paradise. **COSTA RICA**	**WOMEN** **BE AN INFIDEL** **BE FREE - EQUAL** NOT A SLAVE!	You don't have to die to go to Paradise. **ARUBA**

Homosexuals **Have No Home** **In Islam** FORCE ISLAM OUT	You don't have to die to go to Paradise. **BUENOS AIRES**	**HELP US** Drive Out The Evil Forces Of **ISLAM**

Don't Buy Gas From:	Buy Gas From American Co's	Buy Gas From American Oil Companies
Amoco **Chevron** **Exxon** **Marathon** **Mobil** **Shell** **Speedway** **Texaco**	**Arco** **Conoco** **Flying J** **Hess** **Maverick** **Murphy** **Phillips** **Sinclair** **Sunoco** **Valero**	**Arco** **Conoco** **Flying J** **Hess** **Maverick** **Murphy** **Phillips** **Sinclair** **Sunoco** **Valero**
Their Gas Is From OPEC	Keep The $$$ In America	Let OPEC Find A Client Like The U.S.

SUMMARY

Tea Partiers! Because of the challenge I have made to Islam, the Quran and their faulty ideology, I am on their "Hit List." Therefore, I will march on until Chapter 13. **Meanwhile I will have my cohorts out there to help you. I will meet with the Tea Party Headquarters and the candidates for the Presidency until we get to the final rally.**

A Look At The Previous Chapters

In Chapter 8, a question was asked: "Can a Good Muslim Be A Good American?" The answer provided by an expert indicated "NO" in ten separate categories. Also, our train was heading off the tracks.

In Chapter 9, the Challenge was presented. And, in Chapter 10, we have established a plan to Show Islam The Way Out of America. We demonstrate and display the facts on placards that embolden us to charge on because we are right and our rights are being violated by this Administration continuing to appease this evil force called Islam.

Also, our plan will keep the train from running off the tracks and solve the problem as we go.

Sleeping With The Enemy

We have established all the facts bearing on the problem, yet we continue to sleep with the enemy. Why? Because this Administration has no Gonads to do anything about it. They are part of the problem.

We are going to make an impact by rallying our Tea Party Force and arm them with the placards that tell the story about the enemy - Islam. Conventional Wisdom tells us that we can force them out of America with concentrated effort, armed with the truth and persistency.

The Benefits Of Our Plan

Ridding Ourselves Of The Enemy: As I have stated repeatedly in this book, If I Were President, (IIWP), this problem would be solved.

On the other hand, if the President would consider tasking the CIA to look at our findings in this book, and the recommendations that we have made, thus far - that would reinforce our stand against the enemy and we can achieve success in our mission statement.

Stop The Cash Flow To The Enemy: We can start with the gas and oil situation without the help of the Administration. We could rally our forces to boycott all the gas stations in the country that purchase their gas from OPEC. We can also recommend that BP Drill, like the judge said.

Improve Our Economic Posture: Again, IIWP, I would open up drilling opportunities to completely cut off foreign oil purchases. Also, we will get on the Shale Gas Bandwagon.

In addition, we could reduce our minimum wage and increase our productivity of American made goods, thereby increasing jobs, to let the world know that our dollar may not be as strong at the moment, but our buying power is still King.

Secure America: If the government would accept the fact that we are Sleeping With The Enemy, we can remove Islam from within our borders, return our forces home from Afghanistan and Iraq, and conduct war games along our borders. That would be enough to scare anyone away from our borders. Protect the southern border NOW.

Pay Down Our Deficit: It would be long in coming changing the economic outflow with just the forces of the Tea Party, but IIWP, by changing the Administration, we should be able to take care of business ***in a big way - in a big hurry.***

Resolve

The sooner we drive the enemy out of America, the sooner we will be able to regain our posture as the world leader, return the dollar as the standard of world currency, stop the cash flow to the enemy, improve our economic posture, secure our American borders, pay down our deficit and create Jobs for America.

We will overcome! We will Never Surrender! We will rally with the Tea Party Forces armed with placards and signs until every American learn the hard truth about where we are and where we can be with just a little Resolve.

Join Us America! We Will Make A Difference!
DO WE WANT A SAFE AND SECURE AMERICA? THEN, WE HAVE TO GET RID OF THE ENEMY FROM WITHIN.
Origin Of Terrorism – Islam and Saudi Arabia

Chapter 11
America – Take Heed

National Day Of Prayer

In 1952	*President Truman established a day a year as a "National Day of Prayer."*
In 1988	*President Reagan designated the First Thursday in May of each year as the "National Day of Prayer."*
In June 2007	*(then) Presidential Candidate Barack Obama declared that the USA "Was no longer a Christian Nation."*
In 2009	*President Obama canceled the 21st annual National Day of Prayer Ceremony at the White House under the ruse of "not wanting to offend anyone."*
BUT . . .	*On September 25, 2009 . . . from 4AM—7PM*

A National Day of Prayer FOR THE MUSLIM RELIGION was held on the Capitol Hill, Beside the White House. There were over 50,000 Muslims in D.C. that day.

When I started writing this chapter, it was to show the unfairness of the leanings of the President toward Islam over America. But, as I progressed in assembling the facts, I was overcome by emails on the subject. Once I checked them out with Snopes, it changed the direction of this book.

In the spirit of fairness, all the articles are presented in an informational fashion without comments from me.

EXPOSING THE LEFTIST PROGRESSIVE DEMOCRAT MEDIA

In this email, of all the findings on Barack Hussein Obama, the MEDIA SAID THAT IT DIDN'T MATTER.

Obama's grandparents were Socialists who sent his mother to a Socialist school where she met Frank Marshall Davis who was later introduced to young Barack Hussein Obama.

Young Obama was enrolled as a Muslim in school and his father and stepfather were both Muslims.

He wrote in his book that "I will stand with them (Muslims) should the political winds shift in an ugly direction" and admittedly chose Marxist friends and professors in college.

He traveled to Pakistan after college on an unknown national passport. Also, he sought the endorsement of the Marxist Party in 1996 as he ran for the Illinois Senate.

He attended a Chicago Church for twenty years and listened to a preacher spew hatred for America preaching Black Liberation Theology. Later, an independent Washington organization traced his Senate voting record which gave him the distinction of being the most liberal Senator.

To all of this, THE MEDIA SAID IT DIDN'T MATTER.

Please Google:

I'm 63 and I'm Tired by Robert A. Hall.
A Black Man's Point Of View by Lloyd Marcus
Mystery Man President by Wayne Allyn Root
Marxism In America by LTG W. G. Boykin, USA (Ret)
Should Christians Respect Obama? By Dr. David Barton

George W. Bush

Poor President Bush! Since he left office, he has been blamed for everything that didn't quite go the way Obama wanted it to. Here it is, almost three years since he left office, and he's still getting blamed.

Someone wrote a list of things that said, "If George W. Bush: had doubled the national debt, which had taken more than two centuries to accumulate, in one year, would you have approved?

Or, if he had proposed to double the debt again within 10 years, would you have approved?

Or, if he had joined the country of Mexico and sued a state (AZ) in the

United States to force that state to continue to allow illegal immigration, would you question his patriotism and wonder whose side he was on?

Or, if he had put 87,000 workers out of work by arbitrarily placing a moratorium on offshore oil drilling on companies that have one of the best safety records of any industry because one company had an accident, would you have agreed?

Or, if he had spent hundreds of thousands of dollars to take Laura Bush to a play in NYC, would you have approved?

The above are five of 24 questions on the list. But that's enough to make the point. The article closes with: "So, tell me: What is it about Obama that makes him so brilliant and impressive? Can't think of anything? Don't worry. He's done all this in 24 months. You still have another year to come up with an answer.

WHAT HAVE WE LEARNED IN 2,066 YEARS?

"The budget should be balanced, the Treasury should be refilled, public debt should be reduced, the arrogance of officialdom should be tempered and controlled, and the assistance to foreign lands should be curtailed lest Rome become bankrupt. People must again learn to work, instead of living on public assistance."
- Cicero, 55 BC -

EVIDENTLY NOTHING.

Letter From Kitau In Mombasa, Kenya

An email was received that triggered thoughts of serious doubts.

As I read the email, it laid the groundwork to change directions, once again. But, I decided that all that has to be done will be dependent upon honesty and sincerity by the Candidates in the elections of 2012.

My hope was that you will inquire of your Congressman what he knows about the email by Kitau. If he doesn't know, then he should find out what Kitau was talking about.

Impeachment Proceedings? Stop This Train!
Our Country is heading off the track. We have got to fix this problem - in a hurry!

If I Were President - If I were President, I would fix all of this in a great big hurry. But, I'm not. So, we're going to have to take a look at this predicament and take it one step at a time.

The Other Part Of The Disaster

Earlier, we had to do some fast thinking to keep the train from running off the track. This is where the work begins. We have got to find a Conservative who can fix the economy. Taxes must be slashed so that we can encourage entrepreneurs to increase their productivity, bring the jobs back from overseas and put America back to work.

Simultaneously, we need to get the Oil companies focused on opening new drill platforms for exploration and production, thereby creating more jobs.

This Conservative needs the credentials to entice personnel in intelligence, administrations, operations and logistics to straighten out our Social Security System, Health and Personnel issues, local and national security, civil affairs development, and anti-terrorism.

This person must have a will of steel to overcome obstacles few would dare challenge and stare down the opposition knowing that he/she is right. He/she will possess admirable traits to lead and be proud of the accomplishments of its citizens.

The Candidate must be able to attract the rich to join his/her crusade to take the Presidency away from the Liberals and the media. That means raising funds to go against those who supported Obama. Obama still has a trunk full of money left from the previous campaign.

Beating The Odds

The other day, I was listening to Frank Luntz, PhD, on the Sean Hannity Show talking to a group of people about what they thought of the front-running GOP candidates for President in the 2012 elections.

I thought the survey was very interesting So many of them were saying that, "Perhaps it's time to find a candidate who represents the people – someone out of the Beltway – someone who was never in politics – to come straighten out the mess America is in now."

Needless to say, I was thinking the same thing. If Barack Obama could get himself elected with the help of the Media and outside sources with "deep pockets," why couldn't I get myself into that mix?

I won't have the Media, but maybe the Tea Partiers can out-perform the Media. The "deep pockets" will have to be America. I will act as the temporary Chairman to take bids on behalf of the Tea Party as a Candidate. There we have it. It's the Tea Party and America.

Chapter 12
If I Were President

I was saying this all through the book. Then, it made me think that we need this page in this book. I don't have to be the one, but I feel that I could do a better job than Obama.

Tea Partiers: Think of this! If Barack Hussein Obama runs for a 2nd Term as President of the United States, he would be a tough person to beat. He and the media have enough dirt on all our candidates to make us yell, "Uncle!"

I think my plan can beat him.

It doesn't matter about your Party affiliation, whether you are a Democrat, Independent, Republican, Libertarian or Conservative, the biggest problems we are faced with *(that Obama caused)* are: Our Security, Our Jobs and Our Economy.

As President, the Plan in this book will take care of the problems. All we need is the help of the Candidates and people who agree that we need to Fix Our *(Gas Problem)* Economy, Put America Back To Work and Secure Our Borders and the problem is solved.

Here's the Kicker! Google and read the Second Coming of the Mahdi. As President, I will not allow Mahmoud Ahmadinejad or the Muslim Brotherhood to succeed. THEY WILL FAIL!

Can Barrack Hussein Obama say that without lying?
And, I've got "Aces" In This Hand!
Pau! Done! Finis!

As President

I Would Make The Following Items my MISSION STATEMENT:

Secure the Borders - Enforce Immigration Laws
Increase Size of Border Patrol Force – Fly Air Patrol Missions
Conduct Military Training Along the Borders

Force Islam Out Of America
Make arrangements with Saudi Arabia To Take Their Citizens
Back to Saudi Arabia, The Mecca and Medina

Fix The Economy - Reduce Taxes - Increase Jobs
Establish Tax Benefits For Small Business Owners To Increase Jobs
Create Incentive Plans To Bring Their Businesses Back To America

Drill - Drill - Drill
Free America From Purchasing Foreign Oil - Increase Revenues
America has more oil in West US, than all the other resources on Earth.

Eliminate Racial Differences
Too Much Time Is Wasted On Racial Issues
Flights To Be Offered Minorities Who Still Cannot Adjust
Be American or Be Gone

Other Things To Be Accomplished:

War Strategy – Fight To Win – No Dithering
A Fight to Win Policy will be established. An Exit Strategy will also be in place, to ensure that the Combat scene is reestablished.

Cease And Desist Order on Islam
Islam cannot remain in America. After they rewrite their Quran and prove that they are capable of a peaceful coexistence with the other Religions of the World, they may request to return.

No Muslim Can Serve in Our Armed Forces
Since the answer is NO in Chapter8, Can A Good Muslim Be A Good American? no Muslim will be enlisted in the military.

Repeal Obamacare
Rewrite Health Care Plan to help citizens without kick-backs and without taxing citizens out of existence, just to help the 30% who are riding the gravy train (Moochers). Stop that!

Eliminate Czar Positions
All Czar Positions will be eliminated.

Government Pay Structures Adjusted
Pay structures for government employees will be adjusted to be in keeping with the Private Sector.

Reduce Size of Government by 30% Within 2 Years
Consider reducing the number of Senators and Representatives to one-half thereby cutting their staffs.

Review Every Incentive Plan From Departments – Eliminate Waste
Start with Foster Parenting Program

Increase Budget For Defense Department
Combat Readiness will be stressed. Readiness training will be conducted along the borders. Intelligence Gathering will be improved.

Re-establish General Motors and Chrysler As Private Corps

Health Benefits For Politicians Will Be the Same As For All Citizens
"Congress shall make no law that applies to the citizens of the United States that does not apply equally to the Senators and/or Representatives; and, Congress shall make no law that applies to the Senators and/or Representatives that does not apply equally to the citizens of the United States."

Bring Fair Tax Policy To Vote – Eliminate IRS in two years.
Immediately upon approval of the Fair Tax Policy, within the first year, the IRS should be reduced by fifty (50%) percent.

Eliminate TSA
Mayors, Governors and Airports need to work on their airport security.

Eliminate Unions From Government Jobs
Start with the Teachers' Union.

Eliminate Department of Education
Return Education To The States

Eliminate Department of Energy
What have they done to reduce the cost of our gas and oil products?

Abortions Will Not Be Paid For By The Government.
So it is said. So let it be done. Pro-Life Stand.

Move the UN Out Of The US

Ask England To Return The Bust Of Winston Churchill.
It was given as a gift to America, not to Barack Hussein Obama.

Re-Establish The Draft
It's alright to burn the American Flag exercising your First Amendment Right. But, before you do that, you need to serve under the Flag that our veterans have given up so much to keep you Free.

If Under 50 and On Welfare – No Vote – Applies also to Inmates.
Eliminate Moochers. The Liberals can campaign on the issues.

Establish Campaign Reform and Enforce It

Eliminate Welfare Homesteading

End Homelessness In America
Make them a part of the prison system's trustee plan with perks, rather than with money. Work with the Governors to lease property for tent cities and turn criminals into farmers.

Eliminate The Postal System
Meet with CEOs of FedEx, UPS, etc. – to ensure that the private sector can effectively carry our mail system.

No One Will Be Able To Travel With a Hood, Mask or Burka.
No Illegal Immigrants On Welfare or Social Security.
No Illegal Immigrants Registering In American Schools.
No Illegal Immigrants Residing in the United States of America.

Marriage Is Between A Man And A Woman
Since same-sex marriage is against God's plan, why bother getting married? Why go through the courts? Why not just live in sin?

English Will Be America's Spoken and Written Language
Corporations who wish to print translations in other languages may do so as long as they include translations in all languages of the world.

Build The 74-Mile Oil Pipeline To ANWR
Quit dithering. Drop the price of gas now.

Congress Needs To Re-write Retirement Benefits
See Proposed Congressional Reform Act on page 161.

Eliminate the Minimum Wage
We need more products labeled "Made In America." We will reduce our foreign purchases and increase our exports. This is the way we will reduce our deficit to zero. See "Deindustrialization Of America" below. *We can bring all the jobs back to America from overseas.*

Meet With Guest List Personnel and Tea Party Members
Key Personalities (TBA), visit As Often As Time Will Permit.

About The De-Industrialization Of America

The United States has lost approximately 42,400 factories since 2001. Most of those factories employed over 500 people when they were in operation.

Google "De-Industrialization Of America." The author did a great job in assembling the facts that show why America is on a decline and in big trouble trying to help other countries when we cannot help ourselves.

The U.S. Census Bureau says that 43.6 million Americans are now living in poverty and according to them that is the highest number of poor Americans in the 51 years that records have been kept.

How many thousands more factories do we need to lose before we do something about it?

How many millions more Americans are going to become unemployed before we all admit that we have a very, very serious problem on our hands?

How many more trillions of dollars are going to leave the country before we realize that we are losing wealth at a pace that is killing our economy?

How many once great manufacturing cities are going to become rotting war zones like Detroit before we understand that we are committing national economic suicide?

The de-industrilization of America is a national crisis. It needs to be treated like one.

America is in deep, deep trouble folks. It is time we did something about this grave situation.

Add to this list the taxpayer funds doled out to 'preferred' but non-viable green companies. Those companies in turn have sourced their product components from overseas. Think of wind turbine-blades, solar panels, compact fluorescent light bulbs ... most of which are not manufactured in the US. GE has shut down and laid off their bulb-manufacturing operations in the US. 54% of GE manufacturing has now gone overseas!

Why? Because labor is cheaper overseas. We need to eliminate the minimum wage in order to compete with the world.

If left to Obama to solve, this situation will worsen until we have to join the European countries in Surrender.

Can we challenge the power of the Liberal Machine? Please read the Article by Dr. Walter Williams, a Conservative African American, on why Obama will win in 2012. You can Google it.

We Must Challenge The Power! I'll tell you how when we get closer to the end of the road.

Just Under The Wire

During my final editing, I received three emails that I felt I had to include in this book so that I could comment on the contents.

The first email is from a group in Florida who call themselves "GO," but their acronym is really GOOOH, which stands for "Get Out Of Our House." They are attempting something politically radical; getting rid of both parties. They say "We have too many politicians and bureaucrats in Washington and every state capitol who form the "Elite" who care less about you and me, or any of us."

The second email is from Rush Limbaugh commenting about compensations for the victims of the terrorist attack on September 11, 2001 vs. the compensations for our military men and women who were killed in action against a hostile enemy.

The third email (really five – from concerned people) asking about what we're doing in the Middle East. Are you in concurrence with what the President is doing in Libya? Egypt? Mid-East?

From GO:

Politicians do not want you to know they cannot solve the problems in Washington. They know it, and they hope you won't figure it out.

Politicians cannot make the changes that are required to turn things around. They cannot balance the budget. They don't even talk about repaying the $14 trillion we owe. We can bang our head against a brick wall again and again, and it will always hurt.

We can send politicians to Washington election after election, and they will always fail. Or we can tell them to Get Out Of Our House – our House of Representatives.

Politicians have created a political catch-22 from which they cannot escape. The two-party system prevents them from doing what must be done. It forces them to make promises they cannot keep. If one party tries to cut spending the "other" will use it against them. If we continue down this path, our nation will fail.

The solution is to elect leaders who do not care about getting re-elected, do not care about keeping their party in power, and do not care about rewarding those who funded their campaign.

GO has a way to make this happen. Consider this point carefully: **Politicians Cannot Afford To Alienate Voters**. If they do, they cede power to the other party.

Politicians will not (1) pass the 28th amendment that has been circulating for years because it would reduce their power. They will not (2) pass a Fair or Flat tax because it eliminates their ability to reward special interest groups. They will not (3) abolish organizations like the Department of Education because they do not want to alienate the Teachers' Unions. They will not (4) seal the borders because they fear offending Hispanics. They will not (5) reform campaign financing because they need millions of dollars to get re-elected. They will not (6) cut spending because it will cost votes.

Politicians cannot and will not do what must be done.

Both parties claim spending cuts will harm the economy but what has "increased spending" accomplished? Each party has championed massive bailouts, yet the situation has only gotten worse. The two sides are *gridlocked over $60 billion of cuts in a $3.5 trillion budget,* that's like a dieter debating whether or not to eat the last two M&M's in a one pound bag!

Why do we keep sending the same people to Washington? 94% of the politicians in the U.S. House of Representatives will again be re-elected if we do not do something different.

GO offers a solution. Our members will be choosing a candidate to compete in each congressional district in 2012. For the first time ever, Americans will have an honest chance to replace the entrenched politicians. Please get everyone you can to join our movement and elect true representatives of the people who will do the work that must be done.

From Rush Limbaugh

I received an email that was authored by Rush Limbaugh. I agreed with everything he said.

Comments:

To the first email, all the points mentioned have been addressed in this Chapter except one; *the solution is to elect leaders who do not care about getting re-elected.*

Although I agree with it in theory, I think that Rush Limbaugh brings up an interesting point about Congressmen and Congresswomen retiring after one term with $15,000 per month.

I would like to see legislation realigning Representatives' retirement as in the Proposed Congressional Reform Act shown on the next page

Realize, of course, that any politician making such a suggestion *"that a politician should not care about getting re-elected"* could say good-bye to his political career.

Since this Chapter addresses all the points suggested by GO, if I may, GO: consider joining me and the Tea Party to make your suggestions happen.

To the second email, I sympathize with the military families. I am a combat wounded and, sadly, have witnessed too many of our gallant soldiers taken down in harm's way.

I agree with Rush Limbaugh about our politicians serving in the military before sending our warriors into harm's way. Addressing it in this Chapter, I have recommended the reinstatement of the draft.

Also, I think that before politicians consider outrageous compensations, as was the case with the September 11, 2001 attack victims, that whatever compensations that are considered from this point forward should be aligned with the military benefits.

That would mean the cessation of any more benefits for the September 11 families. As for the Oklahoma bombing and embassy bombing victims, the military benefits take precedence. That is to say that any requests for compensations in the future cannot be made in excess of the amount provided to our military families.

If politicians have a problem with that, raise the benefits for our military families.

Proposed Congressional Reform Act
1. Term Limits   12 Years (Possible options below)
   Two Six-Year Senate terms;
   Six Two-Year House terms;
   One Six-Year Senate term and three Two-Year House terms.
2. No Tenure / No Pension: Members of Congress receive a salary while in office. That salary ends when they leave office.
3. Congress members (past, present and future) are to participate in Social Security. All funds in the Congressional retirement fund move to the Social security system immediately. All funds flow into the Social Security system. Congress participates with all Americans.
4. Congress can purchase their own retirement plan, just as all Americans do.
5. Congress will not vote for pay raises. Congressional pay will rise by the lower of CSPI or three (3%) percent.
6. Congress will participate in the same health care system as the American people.
7. Members of Congress must equally abide by all laws they impose on the American people.
8. All contracts with past and present members of Congress are void effective January 1, 2012. The American people did not make the contract members of Congress enjoy. Congress made all these contracts for themselves. Serving in Congress is an honor, not a career. The Founding Fathers envisioned citizen Legislators. Our Citizen Legislators should serve their term(s), then go home and back to work.

To the third email, I am not surprised, at all, by the actions taken by Obama. He was not qualified to be the President when he assumed that role – and, he still isn't.

If I Were President, there would not be American presence in any Mid-Eastern country unless one of them decides to attack Israel;
Shame On Them!

Or if we have another "9-11" attributable to one of them;
Again, Shame On Them!

Or if any of the Mid-Eastern countries request our presence to help them to become Islam-Free.
End of story!

Chapter 13
Saving America

We, The People

America's future depends on us – her people. We can unite as one to take back our rightful place as designed by our Founding Fathers.

It is imperative that the Conservatives design a Plan to take our Country back from the Obama Administration, et al, and then stick to that plan until we get that "wrecking team" out of office.

I've got a plan. It is the best plan on the table. My job is to sell the plan to the Tea Party and America. Take a look and decide.

A Candidate

I know that Obama, with the media, will defeat any of our candidates. BUT WE ARE GOING TO STOP HIM.

America Cannot Survive Another Term Of Obama.

I know, also, that there are many who will disagree with me because our Candidates are all qualified and knowledgeable enough to take the Presidency away from Obama.

Obama has ruined the economy. Joblessness is at 9.2% and rising. He is still pushing to raise taxes and increase the debt limit. Congress is not on his side. It would appear that based on that scenario, he could be defeated easily by any of our Candidates.

Let me present this question for you to ponder. "If we didn't let the Media pick our candidate in 2008, like they did, and went with the top two candidates, Mitt Romney and Mike Huckabee, would we have lost the Presidency?"

Here's another point to consider. I have reason to believe that the Media has already picked our Candidate to run against Obama. If the Media succeeds, like they did in 2008, can we forgive ourselves for losing the Presidency to the Media *(which we are about to do)* again?

The Big Kahuna Plan

So, here's my plan. It is two-fold.

First, the RNC does not name a Nominee – Let the final three Candidates run together as one.

Second, if the final three Candidates can agree to this plan, place me in position, rally around my candidacy, the votes for the candidates will be pooled for KW. We will have a chance at the White House.

The top three Candidates will take turns debating Obama.

I will NOT debate Obama. He is so mendacious, he should be charged with Conduct Unbecoming An Officer in the Military. But, what's the charge for the Commander-In-Chief?

And, besides, with this book in circulation, I will be on the Islam Hit-List, I will surface at the inauguration when Islam should be marching out of America immediately after the ceremony.

As a write-in Candidate, KW will beat Obama! The Candidates will precede me in office for one year at a time. The Media's Republican Candidate would be limited to one year, instead of our losing to Obama.

And the RNC won't have to worry about me. They can help fund the candidates for the Senate so that we can have that in our favor, too.

If the Liberals decide to run someone else in place of Obama, I would still recommend my plan, because we still have to worry about the Liberal Machine. Like I said earlier, as President, our motto, "Be American or Be Gone," will apply to all who oppose America's freedoms.

The Candidates

The Republicans have fielded excellent Candidates for President. Unfortunately, all, except one, are carrying too much baggage.

Let's look at the candidates: Newt Gingrich, Mitt Romney, Ron Paul, Herman Cain, Michelle Bachman. Rick Santorum and now, Rick Perry, and Jon Huntsman – We don't need any more Candidates.

Out of the field, Newt Gingrich is the best qualified. He is brilliant, knows the inner makings of the "Hill" structure and has all the answers.

Sarah Palin, who is not yet a candidate, is the only one who is bullet-proof who can survive the Liberal Machine's attacks. In spite of it, the media, turn-coat Republicans, imitation Conservatives and Liberals, will be shooting at her mercilessly.

My suggestion is to let the Candidates campaign until the number is down to three. Then, we go into action with the "Big Kahuna" Plan.

KW's CANDIDACY

This is not about me. This is about Saving America. I am not a politician, and, I will cede my Candidacy to the Cause. Hence, if nominated, the Candidates will serve in lieu of KW.

    ***"Vote America Back Into Office"* will be our by-line.**

After getting together with the Candidates, who will run the ship, I promise that within the term (or less) America's Super Power status will be restored, our borders will be secured, we will not be dependent on foreign oil, we will resolve the Racial Divide in America once and for all, we will have eliminated Obamacare and reduce the Unemployment rate to two (2%) percent.

Plus, all the tasks outlined on the previous pages will be completed with the help of our advisors, the cabinet, the Tea Party and the leaders that will carry America forward for the next generation who will be a part of the staff before we leave office.

If the media wants to Vet them, they (media) should consider what they are going to tell the American people why they endorsed Barack Obama knowing who he is and what he did.

    America First And Foremost – We Will Not Fail You!

Ponder

Having read "Decision Point" by former President George W. Bush, where he talks about all the mischief he used to get into, my past, that the Media would exploit, if I were a Candidate, would make President Bush look like he was a Choir Boy all his life.

The Media would have a field day. They would make all my little errors in life into a mountain of sin. And, when they're through, why would anyone want to read my book, even if their lives depended on it?

And, talking about the media, we still don't know who Barack Obama is. Isn't that just like the Media? I have countless articles about Obama, some I've shared with you, others I have not verified – then I find out that Snopes is owned by a Liberal. Gosh! Darn!

The Media has picked our Candidate to run against Barack Obama for

2012 by showing that if the election were held today, the candidate would win. *I don't think so. And, I don't want you to buy into that.* There is only one candidate that can beat Obama.

Why We Will Win!

Let me reiterate one point! *Don't let the Media and the Liberals select our candidate like they did in 2008.* Regardless of how the Media juggles the standings of our candidates or endorsing one, like in 2008, my suggestion is to let the candidates campaign until the number is reduced to three, then we swing into action with the Kahuna Plan.

We will let the Tea Party designate the order of their standing. They will take turns debating Obama.

Reviewing my Mission Statement, why would any one vote for us?

The answer is simple. *The Mission Statement contains all the things that the every day, hard working, concerned Americans have wanted for years, but didn't know who to ask to get it done. We will be the "Fall Guys." Blame Us!*

Attack Plan: Eliminate the 15 Trillion Dollar Deficit.

How? By creating an incentive plan for every American to own a piece of America until Congress, can repay them, with interest, for the lending hand.

The Numbers: We will offer the Billionaires, Millionaires and Americans an investment opportunity: Treasury Bonds will be sold at $800 for a return of $1,000 at maturity in 12 months *(plus a bonus repay over the next four years - 100%)* to raise 30 Trillion Dollars. Offer good for U.S. citizens only. *Here is a chance for America's endless ethnicity to excel.* We urge all to pool their resources to capitalize on this offer.

Repayment Plan: By executing the Mission Statement outlined in the previous pages, we should be able to create 20 Million jobs in our first year to generate a cash flow to satisfy our outstanding debt.

Ladies and Gentlemen! Within one year from entering office, we are *debt free* with a Reserve, even after repaying our fellow citizens *(who got richer).* We will pay-off our deficit. *Thank You, America!*

All we need is for the final three candidates to toss their hat in the ring for "KW." Then, they will be in charge of America's future.

This will be a challenge between
Obama and the Media (Deep Pockets) vs. The Tea Party (America)

A Third Party Candidate!

I heard a rumor of a Third Party Candidate. Anyone who suggests running as such in 2012 must be Crazy. It will be a struggle for any Conservative to go head-to-head with Obama. So, the Candidate who dares to run as such, is a fool – another Trojan Horse. No one has the clout to beat Obama as a Third Party Candidate – maybe Bill Gates.

The article by Dr. Walter Williams addresses every possible scenario that one can imagine – whether it be the bad economy, terrible Health Plan, sky-rocketing gas prices, bad decisions made in the mid-east, Obama has no clue about Economics 101, or whatever? - OBAMA WINS!

All the Candidates vying for the Republican Nomination are strong and well qualified. All have the knowledge and platform to turn America around in a big hurry. America would be put back to work.

If it were an election to determine who could best correct the problems that America is being faced with, all caused by Obama, all of the Candidates would beat Obama without question.

Folks! This is not what this election is about. It's all about "Dreams of my Father" and the Liberal Machine, loaded with money, who believe that "dream," and, who has us focused on issues to save our economy. We've got to broaden our focus to include the "far-fetched" dream.

The only way Obama can be beat is for Congress to impeach him now. We've got to pool our resources and provide Congress with the attack cases for Congress to charge him with.

I don't have the resources to beat the Liberal Machine yet. But, with everyone's prayers, as we move ahead, there may be people who really care enough about the freedoms that they have enjoyed here in America up until now, who are concerned about the future for their children and grandchildren, who would pledge their support to "keep America FREE." If so, when the time is right, we will challenge the opposition on behalf of the people of this great Nation to do just that.

A Thought

Think about this! If any of the Candidates opposes this Big Kahuna plan *(because He thinks he can defeat Obama alone – HE CAN'T).* We will have a problem on our hands.

The Media says that 70% of America thinks Obama is on the wrong track. According to Obama's Game Plan, he is right on track. In less than three years, he *(and his team)* has ruined America by design, created 33% Moochers and 16% Hard Core Dems in America.

That is **49%** of the votes. If he encourages **2%** - *(Unemployed drawing unemployment comp, Acorn, Prison reform with tax monies and illegal aliens)*, it will be Dooms Day In America.

By following the Plan, letting the last three Candidates put their "hats in the ring" to campaign for "KW," we can be assured that Our Candidate is in that mix who will be a Special Assistant to the President to help put America back on track. Do I hear an, "Amen?" *Amen!*

If we can do it, I would like to start with Sarah Palin at the helm *(Her selection will become obvious at the end of this chapter)* to get most of the Mission completed. She brings dignity and a "take no prisoner" attitude to the table. The other three will follow.

When we take the White House, you will understand why we need the brilliance and bold attitude in the mix.

In 2016, we will have three or four former Presidents competing to keep the Presidency in the Party.

And Now! We've been told that al-Qaeda is targeting railroad lines all through America as retaliation for the death of Osama bin Laden.

If I were President, al-Qaeda would be non-existent in America – because when we Force Islam Out From Within Our Borders, we will have eliminated all the bases of operations for Terrorists.

Not only that, there would be no questions about our Troops in the Middle-East. They would be ordered home. Iraq and Afghanistan are 97% and 100% Muslims, respectively.

Why are we trying to develop democracy in countries with such a heavy density of Muslims? And, I don't think Afghanistan is worth saving.

We learned that Obama tasked his Administration six times on ways to reduce wastes from all the Departments. DO THEY REALLY WANT TO CUT FEDERAL SPENDING? Ground both Obamas; Eliminate the Czar positions; Eliminate the Energy Dept, Stop promising monies to foreign countries; Stop the Printing Presses; and Stop Obama's Spending. That should balance the budget. *(Almost!)*

Soon, we will be able to identify the three Candidates for our Party. *Our main mission is to take the White House away from Obama. If we fail, I fear that we will see the Late, Great USA bow to Sharia Law.*

However you feel about "tossing your hat in the ring," if you were one of the last three Candidates, can be analyzed later. Right now, by doing that, you are combining the votes of all the Candidates. We can't afford to lose any votes.

While the Campaign is going on, I will be assembling the most brilliant legal minds in America to assist us in ensuring that we will win this race to the White House and the Senate.

Earlier I suggested Palin as a Lead Off ("*Brilliance - No Nonsense*") Candidate to start the cycle when we capture the White House. I think I know who the other Candidates will be.

The "Brilliance and No Nonsense" will continue. That means I will not get a turn as President if asked. *Auwe! (Shucks!)*

Anyway - We Will Win! And, that's the only thing that matters.

America Can Rejoice In Their Renewed Status And Lifestyle Again.

Amen

The Beginning of the End – In Closing

I wrote a letter to my children and their children *(but mailed it to me, if anything should happen to me, then they can have it)* to warn them of the dangers of Islam coexisting with us in America.

Knowing what I know about Islam now, I could not imagine that as a possibility unless we, as Americans, would just lay down our weapons and surrender to them.

Another possibility would be for us to have a leader who had the clout to ask us to do just that, probably in the name of "Political Correctness." A leader who would go so far as to align himself with the other side, then play both sides toward the middle and negotiate a peaceful coexistence on the side of Islam.

The Problem: The letter was written because of the concerns about the bad publicity that would come from this book.

Because of the contents, the flaws of Islam and the flaws of the President, it appeared that I would be *trashed* so that no one would read my book - that is, if I survived the *beheading* by Islam once they learned what I said about their religion.

Trash! It means that every bad thing that I ever did in my life would be made public. It would be dissected to expand its seriousness so that the reader would believe that I was a Scumbag, or worse. I would lose credibility as an author and as a person.

Beheading! Allah, Islam's God, demands beheading of Infidels *(non-believers of the Quran)*. So, I ask you: Does that sound like a religion to you? Would my God ask me to kill anyone who didn't believe in the Bible?

Muslims are discouraged by the Quran to befriend anyone outside of their religion. They are robots who refuse to accept any other points of view. Believing the way they do, they would take offense to the comments I make in the book about Islam. They will be after my head.

Book: The book is about Muslims. After months of TV news on "Terrorism in America," I couldn't understand why our government was having problems identifying the roots of terrorism, which centered on Islam, the Quran and Saudi Arabia. I went to the library for answers.

I disagreed with the Quran's author *(Allah, the Angel Gabriel or Muhammad – pick one)* of what it preaches. Islam is not a religion. I think that Islam is "a massive group of followers of the Quran *(their Bible)* and Shariah Law *(their Constitution).*"

What I learned about Islam and the Quran caused me great concern. So much so, I decided that I had to write about it to let America know who the terrorists were and why America was being targeted. I could see the freedoms that would be taken away from my children and America.

So, the book started out about Islam. It turned more serious when Wahhabism, a much more severe way of Muslim life, came into view. Then, it turned more serious again when it was clearly determined that a "Good Muslim Cannot Be A Good American," *(like Major Nidal Hasan in Fort Hood who shot and killed 13 Military Servicemen).* He was a good Muslim.

While writing the book, there were so many articles crossing the internet about Islam and Politics that interfaced with each other.

There were emails advocating the President: was a Muslim; made a mistake in a speech saying there were 57 States, the number that coincides with the Nations of Islam; he cancelled the National Day of Prayer, but instead had a Day of Prayer for Islam outside of the White House where 50,000 Muslims attended. There were a number of articles suggesting that the economic problem of America was being purposely caused by him.

When a confidential video surfaced about Marxism and the direction that our country was headed, the book turned political and pointed right at the President.

Result: So, based on the fact that the book was focused now on two very serious subjects, I was warned that if the Muslims did not behead me, the forces in our government would destroy me – or make me regret the book was written, and released into circulation.

Decision Making

I had some serious decision-making to undertake. I had to:

Weigh the importance of my life to my children, their children and Americans;

Determine the severity of the threat by Islam who I identified as the "Enemy Within Our Borders;"

Determine the threat by the President with his policies which governs or destroys our country;

Answer a question – Can America Stand Four More Years Of Obama As President;

Another question – What can be done for Muslims who have become "Good Americans?"

Weigh the importance of Islam's doctrines and how it would affect life in the United States;

Big thought – How certain am I that America will become subordinate to Islam / Sharia Law?

Possibilities – If I didn't circulate the book, would the problem take care of itself in time?

Finally - how much of the untold story of my life would I be willing to share with my children?

Facts Bearing On the Problem

Considerations: I have lived a long and enjoyable life. I am the last sibling of a parent, a descendant of the Warrior Prince. I have fifty-three descendants.

The Threat of Islam: If you are not aware of the doctrines that govern the Muslims' way of thinking, you need to educate yourselves.

In the Quran, the author *(Allah, Gabriel, Muhammad)* clearly identify the threat to Muslims as being the Christians. The Christians must be eliminated – beheaded if possible - destroyed until the world is one hundred (100%) percent Muslims.

Currently, there are 2.1 billion Christians and 1.2 billion Muslims; the two largest religions in the world. The other religions of the world in order of size are *Hinduism, Buddhism, Judaism, Sikhism, Baha'iism, Confucianism, Jainism, Shintoism, Zoroastrianism and Taoism.*

The number of Christians in America is declining while the number of Muslims is on a rise. To date, the ten million Muslims in America have been stable. Occasionally, you would read about incidents of harshness by Muslims, who blame the terrorist misdeeds on others.

I am told by my wife that all Muslims are not bad. She knows a lot of Muslims who are really good people. My response to her is that her friends are not true Muslims. If they were, they would not be talking to her. That is the mindset of Muslims. Wahhabism directs other Muslims to kill Muslims who befriend infidels because they, themselves, have become infidels.

The threat Islam poses on America is severe. The severity is explained in the book so that you can plan to protect yourselves.

Can America Stand Four More Years Of Obama?

No! It cannot! If the President survives impeachment charges we (United States) will be delivered to Islam as a Muslim Nation. Our Constitution, which was masterfully scribed by our Founding Fathers, *(that Obama is trying to change)* will be subordinated to Sharia Law. America will have been delivered to the enemy from the "Political Correctness" designed by the Liberal Machine.

What Provisions Can Be Made For Muslims Who Are Good Americans? In the book, there is a recommendation made that can help all Muslims that fall into this category.

How Will America Be Governed Under Shariah Law. The foregone conclusion will be that we have been sold into serfdom.

All the freedoms that we once enjoyed will be gone forever. We will become Dhimmis *(like a slave)* and will have to pay Islam a jizyah *(poll tax)* just to stay alive. Would it be worth it? How can we bear to be employed as a slave, at wages below minimum *(because we were born Americans)* and must pay for the right to eat and breathe in what was once our homeland?

How Certain Am I That America Would Be Subordinated To Islam and Sharia Law? If we do not defeat the Liberal Machine at the polls in November 2012, I am certain, without a doubt, that we will lose our freedoms and the rights to life, liberty and the pursuit of happiness.

The Democrats think they are maneuvering America into Socialism. But, Obama, with his "Dreams Of My Father," has his own plans. He wants to steer America into Marxism, which means that all of our possessions will be taken from us. The most severe loss will be the "right to bear arms."

All weapons will be seized by the US. And, if we haven't removed the UN from the US, then the weapons will be seized by the UN.

Despite the polls, Obama holds a solid 49% lead. He has the money to buy two percent of the votes needed. It is imperative that Congress impeaches him and removes him from office.

Can the problems take care of itself in time?

It doesn't look that way!

Authors: There are many books written on the subject of Islam and the threats they present to the world. Unfortunately, books of that order rarely make it to the top bestsellers. So, in spite of the many publications in circulation, the American public remains uninformed.

What makes me so sure that the public would read my book? I would hope that America would be attentive to the sub-titles of the book –

A Challenge To Islam, Forcing The Enemy Out From Within (Our Borders), Why The Muslim Brotherhood Will Fail. With those sub-titles, the book would be going right at the source of the problem – head on.

Talk Show Hosts: They will talk about the author. They will have fun trying to be the One who pronounces my name correctly.

That may be wishful thinking on my part, but I would hope that the message will flash across the airwaves and get America informed about the contents of the book.

Legislators: Representative King (R), New York, has been a lone voice on the threats of Islam. The Obama Administration probably played politics on the subject. And, Representative King, being weak on firepower, had to work out a deal. *(Translated: He was hushed.)* So, my book will provide fire power to Representative King to pursue the issue among Legislators.

African-Americans: Our biggest threat is African Americans who are converting to Islam. Conversion from Christianity to Islam is at an alarming rate. Based on projections by knowledgeable sources, they predict that, unless this matter is contained, within five years, the number of Muslims will represent over fifty (50%) percent of America's population.

That would mean that they are in a position to vote into office their candidates and their agenda. It would also mean that Sharia Law will be introduced and will replace our Constitution.

My Untold Story

How Much Of My Untold Story Do I Want To Share? The fear is that the "skeletons in my closet," will devastate my children.

Militarily: I enjoyed my life in the military even after the battle scars and heart-aches. Like many of my comrades in arms, I have had to cope with **Post Traumatic Stress Disorder.** From Agent Orange, a defoliant, my illnesses had devastating effects on me. I am a **Disabled Veteran.**

Other Skeletons: I could write a few pages about skeletons. But, they would *PALE* in comparison to the damage that is in your future if Islam is not stopped. Islam is a cancer that has been growing in America for too long and must be removed - NOW.

We've got to get over our "Political Correctness" stupidity and take a good hard look at profiling. We've got to listen to our Intelligence Officers who are loaded with the facts about the Enemy Situation while our leaders are being encouraged from above to ignore the facts.

The Book Is Written — Should It Be Circulated?

Let Me Ask You. How much does your freedom mean to you? Are you willing to gamble that Islam will not seize control of America during your children's lifetime? Can you handle life as a Dhimmi *(slave)*? And pay jizyah *(a fee)* just to eat and breathe?

My hope and dream is that YOU, and the generations of the future, will come to know the freedoms of the world that I grew up in. If the information in the book can spare you your freedoms, I think it will be well worth the challenge to Islam and its flawed doctrines.

A Fight To The End:

With that thought as my guide, I am willing to sacrifice my life for YOUR freedom and for the freedom for all Americans.

To YOU and America - on November 11, 2011 — the publishing company has permission to circulate the book, **"On Guard, America!" (www. onguardamerica.com)**

I have committed myself to this Mission: **To save America from a Take-Over by Islam — By challenging Barack Obama.**

MY CHALLENGE TO ISLAM IS IN CHAPTER 9.

HERE'S MY CHALLENGE TO OBAMA.

Resign Mr. President!

Spare America your plan of destruction. We are on to it and it will not work.

But, if there is grace that can come from what you have done in the past three years — you came close. CLOSE WILL NEVER HAPPEN AGAIN.

The Rest Of The Challenge

Birth Certificate: The green Certificate of Live Birth that Barack Obama provided as proof of birth is not a birth certificate. It is as the name implies. It is proof that the recipient was alive and in Hawaii at the time of issuance. It was issued back in the early 1900s because record keeping could not keep up with the growth at the time.

My Dad received his Certificate of Live Birth when I was six years old. He needed a driver's license and had to prove his name and age.

My birth certificate is in reverse print. My children, who were born in Hawaii, have birth certificates in the same reverse print as mine.

When Barack Obama was born, the certificates issued in Hawaii were still in reverse print – that is to say that the certificate is black with white letters.

Since Hawaii caught up with the times when Barack Obama came along, they should have discontinued the use of the Certificates of Live Birth. I am at odds as to why they were still issuing that certificate at that time.

How Badly Does Obama Want To Stay In Office?

Hawaii could not find a copy of a birth certificate issued to Barack Hussein Obama, II (or Jr).

There are three prominent people who have completed extensive research on the issue of Obama's birth certificate. They have proven, beyond a doubt, of his birthplace - which was not in the US – especially, not in Hawaii - that would jeopardize Obama's Presidency, as it should.

If, by chance, those people, and me, turn up missing, for no reason at all, I have their names recorded. It would be interesting to see to what extent the responsible perpetrators would go to cover up this issue.

Covering up this issue will not be in the best interest of anyone who is thinking along these lines before or now.

I am not a racist, but I don't mind being one if that's what it's going to take to get this Birther issue resolved once and for all.

Get Busy, Congress!

I shouldn't have to show my birth certificate. It's Obama's birth certificate you need to see. Impeach Barack Hussein Obama – NOW!.

We need for all the Talk Show Hosts and the Tea Party to rally with their "talking points" to get this Birther issue resolved once and for all.

It's time to stop playing games and get serious about fixing America's problems caused by the Impersonator-In Chief. Let's Unite and take back the Oval Office.

We need investigations conducted to identify all the people who knew about this scam that propelled Obama into the Presidency.

We also need to identify the people who prospered by Obama's purposely destroying the economy of the United States from 2008 until 2011, or when Obama is actually stopped and replaced.

Turn The Clock Back To 2008

Congress: From the issue at hand, we should turn the clock back to 2008. Since Congress is a legitimate body, but the Obama-Biden Ticket is not, the records should show that, once the Birther issue is resolved, the Presidency should be, instantly, terminated and the Presidency reverted to the rightful winners of the Race, McCain-Palin. And, from that point in time until November 2012, they are the occupants of the White House.

It means that all documents signed by Barack Obama would be null and void. That includes, of course, Obamacare, all the new regulations that stunned the growth of our economy, and his latest scam to offer illegal immigrants amnesty so that he could remain President in 2012. Add to that the two appointments to the Supreme Court.

For the sake of the 2012 election, I would recommend that McCain does not try to further his political career. He was the Media's Candidate in 2008.

In spite of the Media's prediction that it would be an easy win for the Democrats, they (Dems) came close to losing it with the gutsy show of force displayed by Sarah Palin. If McCain had left her alone, she was perched to turn the McCain-Palin Candidacy into a big Win.

With that said, he (McCain) should be satisfied to have made it to the top to become the oldest President. Be happy with that - retire in 2012.

But, for Sarah Palin, history cannot deny her. She can take her rightful place as Vice-President and gather the candidates for the 2012 elections to help her form the new Administration to bring America out of the hole we are in. I trust that she can, in a relatively short period of time, with the help of the Candidates, move America back into world prominence.

The New Administration

Once the new Administration settles in after celebrating the change, I would hope to see them "grab the bull by the horns" and run the enemy out of town.

If you have problems with believing that Islam is the enemy within our borders, ponder with this thought.

Barack Obama was put in place by the powers (not yet fully identified and eliminated) to turn America into an Islamic state. The Liberal Machine thought he was just going to move toward Socialism, but, if he had succeeded, America would have been converted to an Islamic Nation with Shariah Law; our freedoms replaced by serfdom.

Accept the facts and take action to return our nation to the way our Founders meant it to be.

But It's Not Over Yet

There are a lot that has to be done for us to get past the activities that took place between 2008 to present. The previous occupants of the White House left an ugly mark recorded in our history books for the past three years that must be corrected.

It is my hope that every penny raised by Barack Obama for his campaign after becoming President be used to defray the cost of expenses for all the vacations and shopping sprees made by him and his wife during 2008 to present.

I would also hope that everyone who was an accessory to the fact, that Obama had flaws in his record making him ineligible to serve as President of the United States of America, be held accountable.

No one, especially Barack Obama, should leave office with a penny more than they had when they arrived in office.

Let the records show that America was put at risk by the Liberal Machine with an imposter at the helm. Let America know how close they came to being made serfs by Islam at the request of the Chief Imposter.

The Liberal Machine vs. Congress

Assuming that the Liberal Machine is stronger than I have assumed it to be, and they manage to squelch the "Birther Issue," here's what we still have going for us.

We should march on with the Big Kahuna Plan. The campaign will be about the Liberal Machine and Obama, which must be defeated.

We should go into a massive fund-raising program using my multi-cultural back-ground to attract Europeans, Hispanics, Asians, Pacific

Islanders and the world to help us Win the White House for them, as well as for us.

We should encourage all the Muslims who wish to stay in America to join the Arabian Faith. They can be assured of their place in America's future, pledging their allegiance to help us defeat the Liberal Machine.

We should make an offer, a Fair Tax Plan, to the Corporate CEOs who are headquartered outside the US of the advantages of returning their offices to America.

We should let Saudi Arabia apologize for being the enemy and come in peace to help our cause to defeat this Liberal Machine.

We should also ask Japan to have their JAL Airlines, who partnered with "1250 Oceanside Partners," to cease their construction at Hokuli'a in Hawaii, my ancestors' burial site, and to help us instead. They will be glad they did.

Coupled with our Allies, of whom we are grateful, and the Axis of Evil - lending a hand, the world will be at peace. We can forge ahead on a course for eternal World Peace.

END?

This

Is Just

The Beginning!

ON GUARD, AMERICA

Forcing The Enemy Out From Within

A Challenge To Islam

Why the Muslim Brotherhood Will Fail

Because of the Political contents of this book, there will be Updates that will be released monthly *(to Purchasers of the Book)* between now and Election Day, November 2012.

(Be sure to leave us your email address when you purchase a copy of this book.)

Each Update will be a Challenge To Obama of Impeachable Offenses – Once he has been impeached, the Updates will cease.

Let's not lose sight of the purpose of this book – "Forcing The Enemy Out From Within."

Our Freedoms are at Stake!

Another thing - This Administration is spending monies we don't have rebuilding Mosques in the Mid-East.

What???

Autographed Copies Of This Book

Tea Partiers: Please read page 138. I don't know how long I will be able to stay invisible.

I need your help:

1. To circulate this book; and,
2. To encourage requests for autographed copies of the book.

Circulation: If you can ask your friends to get a copy of this book, and everyone does the same thing, the Conservatives all over America will be informed in a relatively short period of time.

Autographed Copies: Go to www.onguardamerica.org and purchase five books from Authorhouse.com, then fill out the bottom of the form (name, address, email, etc), and submit your request. I will mail you an autographed copy of the book and a note of (*Mahalo*) appreciation.

You can give the five books to your family or friends. If anything happens to me, you will have a treasure – double your investment.

A Chance To Meet: When we force Obama out of office, we will ask former Governor and Vice-Presidential Candidate Sarah Palin and Congresswoman and Presidential Hopeful Michelle Bachmann to arrange a time and place to gather so we can thank you for your help.

ON GUARD, AMERICA
A Challenge To Islam

- Forcing The Enemy Out From Within -

Why The Muslim Brotherhood Will Fail!

Kalai-o-Waha

PAU!

ALOHA

CPSIA information can be obtained at www.ICGtesting.com
Printed in the USA
LVOW101002290212

270858LV00001B/5/P